Investigating Mathematics

by
Howard Zeiderman

Publisher - CZM Press
Printer - C. Colby

ISBN 1-878461-20-6

Copyright 1994
by CZM Press
48 West Street #104
Annapolis, MD 21401
Second Printing 1996

[Permission to reprint other copyrighted texts which have been used in this
volume has been applied for and explicit acknowledgements will be printed in the
next edition.]

Acknowledgements

Any work which maps out a new direction is always a cooperative effort. As ideas germinate, they invariably draw on the experiences and reports of many people. As thoughts are first articulated, discussions ensue. I first wish to thank the students who participate in the Touchstones Discussion Project. Their ability to investigate the mathematics and science texts included in the Touchstones series confirms our belief that at the deepest levels mathematics is a discussable human activity. Over the years, these results were explored by me along with my colleagues at Touchstones, Geoffrey Comber and Nicholas Maistrellis. They and Steven Werlin encouraged the direction I pursued, offered suggestions and ideas, proposed new approaches, did heroic editorial work in reading early and late drafts, and gave invaluable advice. I also thank Austin Zeiderman, my son, a member of the proposed audience for this volume, for his thoughtful insights and his careful and critical reading of the volume. Colleen Daly and her assistant Hannah Gillelan were always patient and good humored as they typed and formatted the volume, and monitored the ever-increasing files which strained their memories, mine, and the computer's. This second edition has benefitted in important ways from the thoughtful editorial suggestions of Janice Cater. Authors become so familiar with their own work that even obscure passages appear transparent. Janice invariably spotted these and consistently recommended ways to make them clear. The work has greatly gained from her contributions and the editorial labors she and Geoffrey Comber shouldered. I also thank Thomas Wilson for his inspired title for the unit on the perfect languages, and Margaret Winter for her daily encouragement and faith in this project. This work represents the belief of all of us that students of all ages respond in remarkable ways when respectfully challenged.

H. Zeiderman

Table Of Contents

Foreword

Investigating Mathematics has been designed first and foremost as a supplement to regular mathematics classes. The thinking that underlies it is explained in the *Introduction*, which is followed by a section describing how to use the book. These two sections form an important part of the book, and should be read by students and teachers alike. No separate period need be set aside to discuss the issues these sections raise. Although principally intended for use within a discussion format, this volume can serve as a reader for anyone wishing to investigate the nature of mathematics as a human activity.

INTRODUCTION

"That's right." "That's wrong." How many times have we heard or used those expressions in a mathematics class? Most frequently in our everyday lives, answers are better or worse, rather than right or wrong. This is also sometimes true in other classes in school: in English and social studies classes, even once in a while in science courses. Mathematics, however, appears to be a realm unto itself. It's the place where everything looks certain, where there is rarely room for discussion, and where a question more often means we haven't caught on rather than that we are curious. In mathematics classes, human motives, decisions, and choices appear absent. However, larger and smaller infinites and the $\sqrt{-3}$ are as common as the triangles and counting numbers we were familiar with even before we came to school.

Mathematicians realize that this misrepresents their subject matter by presenting a very one-sided view. Though an important goal of mathematicians is to discover and create a field of study where every question has an answer and where every statement is supported by reasons, this finished product distorts what lies behind and beneath it. The actual work of mathematicians is filled with uncertainty, and with explorations which sometimes are fruitful, sometimes barren. Discussions among mathematicians to articulate approaches and strategies that are better or worse play an essential role in their efforts. Though some mathematical questions seek information, many seek rather to open new lines of investigation. Analogies from experience, our very human desires for beauty and simplicity, and decisions and choices about what is more or less important pervade the activity.

To isolate these foundations and underlying components from the theorems, formulas, and technical manipulations presented in textbooks makes the content of geometry, algebra, number theory, logic, and calculus appear unnecessarily alien and arbitrary. Dealing with imaginary numbers like $\sqrt{-3}$, or comparing differing infinites, takes on either the merely game-like character of following seemingly arbitrary rules or an alien and mystical dimension which eludes our understanding. When we try to grasp an imaginary number, we find ourselves frustrated because we know no more about it than that certain rules apply. When we ask ourselves what the $\sqrt{-3}$ is, we feel unsatisfied and confused when all we can say is something like, "Two of them multiplied together result in -3." If, however, we both broaden and deepen our investigation, we begin to demystify mathematics and humanize it. If we ask why a mathematician would take such a step, if we ask what the gains and the costs of using imaginary numbers might be, we enter the more recognizable realm of human goals and decisions.

1

All of us make generalizations from our experiences. Sometimes these are useful; sometimes they are harmful. In every instance there is a price to pay. When we generalize, we either minimize how our experiences differ from one another in order to focus on how they are the same, or we highlight the difference and neglect the similarity. Sometimes, as we all are aware, the gains outweigh the costs. Mathematicians are no different from the rest of us. If we explore the gains they pursue, the costs they are willing to endure, and the particular options they choose, we find ourselves on more familiar ground. *Investigating Mathematics* charts a course to this realm of thinking. Through this journey, mathematics will appear less arbitrary and mysterious. It will also be more engaging because we will do more than absorb mathematical results; we will participate in the human activity called mathematics.

Textbooks are the central feature of mathematics courses, and always should be. Mathematics textbooks present work that has already been investigated. Their task is to refine and organize a subject matter that has achieved a high degree of acceptance and utility among mathematicians and scientists. They transmit information to us. They attempt to incorporate the most efficient method for us to master the material of a specific subject. Textbooks explain; they don't create. The author is an expert on a topic, generally created by others, and the teacher is the local representative who transforms a work written for all students into one that addresses the particular needs of a specific class. Textbooks place us solidly and almost exclusively in the realm of correct and incorrect answers, proven approaches, and plausible strategies. Examples from our experience play a secondary role. At most, they illustrate technical materials, concepts, theorems, and problem-solving techniques in order for us to follow the presentation more adequately. Textbooks are an essential component of learning mathematics, and other subjects often strive to imitate their form and ideals. Textbooks need to be supplemented, however, by different kinds of materials, materials that encourage students to think mathematically, to think as mathematicians.

This book is that supplement. *Investigating Mathematics* contains sixteen units. Each unit begins with an orientation section, which raises general concerns that always occur within mathematical exploration. This is followed by a short original text in which a mathematician creates a particular field of mathematics or a new approach to the entire subject. Each unit opens up for investigation the fundamental issues and decisions that textbooks, from the nature of their particular task, presuppose. For those who use this book in a mathematics class, the investigation will take the form of a group discussion. Those who use this book as a reader will carry on this investigation on their own.

The orientation section supplies the compass points of options within which particular mathematical decisions have been made. It sets the stage for reading the mathematical text, and, along with the text, encourages the multiplicity of perspectives needed for the discussion. The orientation section presents the general issues that surround a particular mathematical approach by setting out part of the familiar, everyday framework that incorporates comparable concerns. In addition, each orientation section acquaints the reader with certain concrete technical issues in the text. It is neither an explanation of the text nor a commentary. Instead, it tries to prepare the reader to come to terms with the way in which familiar human decisions and attitudes take mathematical shape.

The original texts in the volume are not presented to supply historical background. Rather, the texts that first open up a field of mathematics are a unique resource. In them, mathematicians expose the purposes, choices, gains, costs, and strategies that come to pervade the subject matter. In these texts, mathematicians carve out a new region of exploration. In each case, they enter an uncharted land where they themselves, as the first explorers, must place landmarks for others to follow. These landmarks are fashioned from their own previous experience. Though some of this experience is of previous mathematics, most of it comes from the experiences mathematicians share with non-mathematicians.

In creating a new approach or a new field of mathematical investigation, the central insight can only come from a new perspective. Were this perspective already mathematical, one would have only a further refinement of a well-mapped area. It would be like repaving a road or widening it, rather than like opening a path that no one has ever travelled. In this regard, the texts, though mathematical, are like poems; the mathematicians are like poets, who must forge images and metaphors from their most human experience in order to extend the horizon of our thinking. Surprisingly, although these decisive works, like all of mathematics, have a technical component, they are essentially non-technical. The work carried out in these texts precedes the highly technical work that is set out in textbooks. The pieces in this volume first establish the techniques that the textbook development of their subject matters requires. To achieve this, they must raise — sometimes explicitly, though most frequently implicitly — the kinds of questions that engage all thoughtful human beings. These are questions such as:

- How do we achieve certainty about our beliefs?
- How much can we trust our experience and our imagination?
- What does it mean to understand something?
- What is the relation among the different kinds of things we know?

These questions, which pervade and animate the mathematical decisions in these texts, transport us from the realm of correct and incorrect answers to a region where answers are better or worse. It is an investigation in which students who have some proficiency in mathematics, but who represent a wide range of confidence, fear, and ability, can and should participate.

Probing and retracing this territory requires a new form of guidance, a different mode of teaching. Discussion, rather than lecture, is the appropriate way to reanimate the choices and purposes embedded in these texts. Lectures are useful when correct information is the crucial issue. When, however, there is no unambiguously correct answer, lectures curtail investigation. To explore these issues requires the diverse perspectives of all the students and the teacher. Discussion is the only route in which these can become available. All the vastly different skills of people are needed to uncover the original paths that lie underneath the current highways of mathematics. Students with abilities in literature and social studies must cooperate with those whose strengths are in mathematical strategies and problem-solving. The former see more acutely the alternatives that might have led to different paths, the options these mathematicians decided not to pursue. The more mathematically able are more aware of the mathematical structure that came to be constructed once a particular path was cleared. The original thinkers whose works we will discuss had nothing but a kind of intellectual compass to assist them in their exploration. This volume contains these compasses in orientation sections which precede each text.

The orientation section looks at general and fundamental mathematical issues from a contemporary vantage point. It presents themes that are threads through the accompanying text. The texts, on the other hand, present these issues in a concrete shape and from a different and often non-contemporary perspective. The texts exemplify the issues raised in the orientation section, and act to focus the discussion. But the texts offer more than the specific approach that the orientation section develops. It is a sustained exploration of a topic. Additional issues arise in the detailed articulation of the investigation it pursues. Although the discussion should begin within the context of concerns spelled out in the orientation section, it could well depart widely by pursuing other topics or images raised in the texts. Remember, a discussion is not intended to cover material but to explore it. And exploration always takes unpredictable directions.

This volume is for both the teacher and the students, who must bring their differing backgrounds, perspectives, and skills to the endeavor. The result of this investigation will be both a deeper understanding and greater confidence towards mathematics, as well as the recognition that mathematics is a deeply human activity.

How To Use This Volume

Who Should Use This Volume?

Investigating Mathematics is designed primarily for high school students in grades 11 and 12, though some 10th and 9th graders will also find it useful. The students who will gain most from it are those who have demonstrated some competence with geometry and algebra. Those students who are already able to think about specific topics in mathematics will be taken to the next step. They will learn to think mathematically, to think as mathematicians think. As a rule of thumb, students who have a B or better average in mathematics are the intended audience. Two other groups of students, however, who have not achieved this average, can also gain from this work.

Some students, who are mathematically able but, because it comes easily, don't make an adequate effort, are other candidates for this volume. They begin to take the subject more seriously when confronted with more complex issues, issues that go beyond the mere technical facility that they sometimes scorn. Though not intimidated by mathematical symbols and techniques, such students are often apathetic. They see mathematics as a game that they sometimes wish to play, but, at other times, don't because they lack the inclination. These students frequently take their own abilities more seriously when they realize that beneath and surrounding mathematical manipulation are serious issues, which require thoughtfulness rather than unusual technical facility. *Investigating Mathematics* forces us to reflect on our mathematical and intellectual presuppositions. This self-examination and criticism often acts as an antidote and corrective to the complacency which such highly able students display.

The third group are those who have been alienated from mathematics but who display skill and ability in other subjects, particularly literature and poetry. Such students have often developed an antipathy towards and even a fear of a subject in which arbitrariness and mere correctness seem to rule. They are distanced from mathematics by its apparent isolation from more recognizable, more ambiguous, and more engaging human concerns. *Investigating Mathematics* can act as a bridge into regular class work for these students. By stressing the fact that the issues that concern them in poetry and literature also pervade mathematical decisions, this bridge can give mathematics a less alien appearance. By highlighting the deeply human nature of mathematical thinking, it can help such students begin to feel they are on familiar ground.

These three groups will all gain from the explorations provoked by the Touchstones approach.[1] The three threads of the effort that respectively affect these groups are:

1) Mathematics is a creative act requiring decisions and initiative.
2) Mathematics involves self-examination of presuppositions and intellectual biases.
3) Mathematics is a deeply human activity.

When to Use This Volume:

Investigating Mathematics is a supplement to a normal mathematics curriculum. Each unit consists of an orientation section, an original text, and a set of questions which the students prepare before class. The discussion of the unit generally lasts one class period, though each unit could easily sustain more than one class meeting and/or be followed up by a longer written assignment. The sixteen units of the volume are independent of all specific course content. Each raises issues that pervade all mathematical activity. The units can be regularly scheduled through one year, or used as an occasional supplement. The former option would involve one meeting every two weeks, the latter would clearly depend on the time available. Some schools may wish to use the volume in a voluntary after-school activity or as an elective eight to ten week course. Such a course would require approximately three meetings per week and could involve longer writing assignments after the discussion sessions have occurred. If the volume is used regularly, the sequence of units should be followed. Though the units are independent of one another and self-contained, certain issues would be more profitably considered before others. For example, it would be appropriate to consider the role of definitions in mathematics which happens in Unit I, before discussing what an axiom should contain in Unit XII. This sequence is useful, however, not because the topics are cumulative. Rather, it is because issues that emerge in one lesson can usefully re-emerge in exploring other topics. It is perfectly possible to modify the order, because each unit contains its own adequate materials and resources for a fruitful discussion. The order presented in this book is a suggestion, rather than a firm requirement.

Teachers who elect to use the volume with their students less regularly should consult the Appendix. You will find short summaries of each unit, and suggestions about possible sequences in terms both of difficulty and topics.

---

[1] The Touchstones Discussion Project began in 1985 and currently involves 250,000 public and private school students of all abilities and backgrounds. Through regularly scheduled discussion classes, students develop radically new and complex skills of thinking, communication, and self-reflection. Through Touchstones, students cease being merely good or bad students. They learn how to teach others and teach themselves.

Some teachers may decide to use this volume as a reader for themselves or for individual students whom they feel might gain from it. Many people have reported that the volume increases their level of comfort with mathematics even when the reading does not culminate in a group discussion. English and social studies teachers will find themselves less alienated from what is often conceived as a dry and austere subject. English teachers become more open to using analogies from these texts when presenting topics in literature. Social studies teachers will become more able to bring up issues about technology and about mathematics in exploring the social, historical, and political dimensions of events. Science teachers will notice many parallels to issues in physics, chemistry, and biology. Mathematics teachers will find they are more able to inject topics for discussion into their regular course work.

The Stages of Each Unit

A. Preparation:

Preparation for class involves reading the entire unit – the orientation section and the text – and writing responses to the questions. This preparation will require approximately two hours. Preparation for this class meeting, however, differs from normal preparation. **The material is not meant to be mastered: students are not meant to solve problems or prepare definite answers to questions teachers might ask. Instead, preparation involves becoming familiar with an issue and thoughtfully considering one's attitude about it. The material in each unit is not meant to be covered, but thought about and explored. Don't worry if there are passages which are confusing. You will often need one another's assistance to clarify issues and approaches.**

The Orientation Section - This section presents an issue that is both fundamental to current mathematics and also to a variety of other subject matters and human activities. Examples of these are: how we use metaphors, what maps and models are, and whether mathematics is a perfect language and an ideal we should strive for in other contexts. The orientation section orients the reader; it is a compass which directs further exploration. It is not principally a commentary or explanation of mathematical concepts, though it contains some of this. Insofar as it offers commentary or explanation, the points it raises are invitations to disagreement and discussion. By presenting the ambiguities in concepts, strategies, and general approaches, it supplies the context for examining the presuppositions embedded in textbooks. The orientation section reveals the fact that intellectual investigation in mathematics depends on a variety of decisions and choices about what is more or less important. It therefore makes visible the goals and purposes of mathematics, and invites consideration of how these goals reinforce or conflict with other human goals.

The Text - Each unit contains a mathematical selection or excerpt that presents a decisive event in mathematics.[2] The orientation section will indicate when the text should be read. Generally it is read after the orientation section. Occasionally, it is read at a particular stage of the orientation. These texts opened new fields of mathematical thinking, reinterpreted previous mathematics, or offered a new perspective on mathematics. On the whole, they are non-contemporary texts, the so-called "classics" of mathematics. They are not, however, presented as resources in the history of the subject; their historical characteristics are not at all important for us here. Rather, they are used to reveal the sources and genealogies of the assumptions of contemporary mathematics, assumptions which are raised in the orientation section.

Though these texts very from the completely non-technical, as in Pascal, to the highly technical, as in Hilbert, they are fundamentally untechnical. As the initiators of certain directions in mathematics, their authors present examples of what they propose mathematics should be like. In this sense, the technical side of mathematics and the attitude it exemplifies are still at issue. In contrast to the way we study mathematics textbooks, where the technical procedures are to be mastered, the readers should approach these texts as critics and judges. The technical aspects of a text – in Hilbert's axioms, for example – are simply that author's suggestion. They propose a view of what mathematics is. These texts, therefore, become the opportunity for us to evaluate the gains and costs of such an attitude intellectually, rhetorically, and emotionally. In other words, they enable us to recognize and discuss which texts would be accessible to most literate readers and which require specialized background. This difference highlights the question of mathematics as a human activity. The texts, therefore, make concrete the general issues raised in the orientation section. The mathematicians who wrote these texts were struggling to articulate an idea. The struggle makes visible the goals and liabilities of a certain approach. Though these texts are excerpts, there is no more extensive body of information that justifies the various approaches. Insofar as it appears that an author makes certain assumptions, those very assumptions should be articulated, explored, and evaluated.

The Questions - The best way to determine our attitudes toward issues, problems, approaches, and strategies is through writing. The questions which are included in each unit are geared to elicit these. These questions, unlike those in textbooks, do not have correct or incorrect answers. Rather, they focus on our attitudes or beliefs

---

[2] Most of the texts are continuous extracts from original texts. Some have been adapted for the purposes of this volume. In the latter cases, multiple lines of thought were simultaneously pursued by an author. A single thread, appropriate to the particular issue raised in the orientation section, was extracted. This required editing and adaptation.

concerning a variety of issues about which we may not even realize we hold definite opinions. Responding to the questions does not involve searching through the orientation section or the text for an appropriate passage, one which will supply an answer. It involves determining whether our reaction to the attitudes and viewpoints expressed in the orientation section and text was positive, negative, or neutral. We must then ask ourselves to articulate some more general reasons or attitudes, often stemming from our opinions about non-mathematical issues that underlie our reactions. These responses should be kept in a small journal notebook and brought to class. They will supply the starting points for exploration through discussion.

B. The discussion:

The Class Meeting - The class meeting is intended as one class period, approximately 40-60 minutes in duration. In certain instances a group or the teacher will feel they should spend another meeting on the same unit, and will have the time for this activity. Each unit can usefully sustain a discussion for more than one meeting, though this is not an expected practice. Using *Investigating Mathematics* assumes a level of maturity that few other programs require. It does not assume extraordinary levels of mathematical facility. Approximately 25% of all students will find themselves capable of preparing the material adequately for the discussion. It does, however, assume that students will make the effort to cooperate with their teachers for the success of the activity. The class meeting will utilize a discussion format. Unlike regular classes, which principally involve the presentation of material in a clear and interesting manner by a teacher, discussion requires that all participants contribute. The degree of success of the discussion cannot be guaranteed by the skill and interest of the teacher, but only by the willingness of mature participants to take on new responsibilities. This requirement is made explicit by the fact that there is no special teachers' edition of *Investigating Mathematics*. All participants use the same volume.

If you do not elect to spend a class meeting considering the introduction and the previous section on the use of the volume, you should make time in the first session to consider the following points to be raised about the discussion process.

The Discussion Format - The orientation section and the text do not supply material to be covered or gotten through. The questions they raise do not have right or wrong, correct or incorrect answers. The answers they seek are responses that may be more or less well justified. The material is explored to determine the gains and costs of a specific approach or set of assumptions. In short, there is very little information to be conveyed, and discussion is the appropriate form for these other activities. In our experience of leading discussions in many diverse contexts and developing in teachers and students the skill to lead or participate in them, we have discovered a number of surprising characteristics of the activity. The first and most crucial one is that our normal expectations and predictions about who will be good or not good at discussions are often inaccurate. You should be prepared to be surprised. Every member of a discussion group has skills as well as weaknesses.

Highly articulate people can present their own thoughts clearly and engagingly. However, often these very people find it difficult to allow others to finish their own sentences. They imagine they understand another's opinion even before it's completely stated. The result is that they frequently misinterpret a different perspective. On the other hand, students who are shy and appear withdrawn, and who often stumble at expressing themselves frequently have high listening skills. They really do hear what others say. It is clear what each member of these two groups will have to strive for. Those who speak readily will have to discipline and restrain themselves to make room for others. Those who are hesitant about speaking in a public setting will have to muster up the courage to speak. Each of you has a unique perspective on the issues to be explored. The issues are mathematical, but they also range beyond mathematics into other subjects and experiences. Each of you will have a valuable response to contribute. Everyone is hesitant to speak publicly and make errors. Obviously, no one enjoys the kind of embarrassment where one appears foolish. This, however, will not occur in these discussions. Your responses and comments are not right or wrong, correct or incorrect. The only reason for embarrassment in such a discussion is speaking thoughtlessly, and thoughtlessness merits embarrassment.

The following aspects of discussions should be kept in mind:
1. Arrange the chairs in a circle. It is difficult or impossible to have a discussion facing the back of someone's head.
2. Avoid side conversations with your neighbor. Imagine that *you* are speaking, and suddenly a few others begin speaking to their neighbors. You would probably feel offended, thinking that they didn't care about what you had to say. Probably you would not speak as readily in the future.
3. Silences occur in discussion. Don't expect the teacher to break the silence for you. Silences are not so terrible: people need time to think. Also, a silence often makes room for new speakers, particularly those of you who have some hesitations about speaking in a large group.
4. A discussion is not an argument or a debate. When people begin participating in discussions, they often think the purpose is to argue with others and defend their own points at all costs. This frequently results in a kind of ping-

pong match where the ball is hit back and forth endlessly between two people or groups. The others become mere spectators. They are often amused at first by the drama of an argument, but, like all mere spectators, they eventually become bored. A discussion is an exploration, though on occasion an argument will develop. When it does, and when the argument seems to be going nowhere except into a battle of wills, let it drop.

5.   These meetings end at the bell. In regular classes, there is often closure. The teacher summarizes what was covered. Any such summary of a discussion is artificial and will misrepresent it. A discussion will not generally reach a conclusion or achieve a consensus. This can be frustrating, but is an important dimension of exploration.

6.   If you bring up background information about a subject or issue, it is your responsibility to make it available as briefly as you can to everyone in the group. Generally, such information is not useful. It merely presents second-hand reports, and it avoids the more serious task of thinking about what is confronting everyone present. In short, it is merely a disguised assertion of power and authority, which is hardly helpful in a discussion among equals.

Other problems about the process will undoubtedly emerge and should be solved by the group as a whole. One example is whether to raise hands. Raising hands to speak is a habit we all have in school situations. The advantage is that it is an orderly method of procedure. The disadvantage is that someone, perhaps the teacher, will then have to call on people. Speaking without raising hands, which is typical in the **Touchstones Discussion Project,** is initially disturbing. Multiple conversations emerge simultaneously. Participants quickly learn, however, to anticipate who is trying to speak and to act as a group in a cooperative effort to make room for one another. Your group should decide which option you prefer.

A discussion can be fruitful and exciting, but is difficult and can be frustrating. It requires courage both to speak publicly and also to listen carefully to others who may disagree with you. Keep in mind, however, that each writer you will read took great risks in venturing out into an uncharted realm of mathematical thought. You should be willing to respect their efforts enough to take a similar risk in thinking about the advantages and disadvantages of their efforts.

IS IT JUST A MATTER OF DEFINITION?

I

TEXTS: Euclid, *Elements;* Plato, *Meno;* and
Wittgenstein, *Philosophical Investigations.*

Orientation:

In many of the dialogues written by Plato, Socrates invites others to seek a definition. Often at the start of a Platonic dialogue, someone will make a claim about an important subject – about knowledge, honor, friendship, justice, or excellence. Rather than disagree, Socrates will innocently ask what knowledge or justice means, what its definition is. He is asking what is the same in all cases of knowledge or justice. This step probably seems familiar and obvious to all of us. Undoubtedly many of us have asked others, and have been asked this Socratic sort of question. It is difficult from our perspective to appreciate just how revolutionary this simple question was. Yet the Platonic dialogues, written about 375 B.C. in Athens, are the first evidence we have of seeking, proposing, and evaluating definitions. In earlier texts from all cultures, there is no evidence that definitions were investigated or employed. So much of our lives is determined and influenced by specific definitions– both by learning definitions and by seeking them – that the shock and confusion often caused in the dialogues by Socrates' question is itself shocking. Many of the people he interrogates don't quite understand what he is after, and he must make considerable effort to explain what a definition even looks like.

For us, definitions are part of the fabric of our lives. We have all felt the need while reading a book or writing a paper to look up a definition. Most of us have probably felt excluded from an activity because we didn't satisfy the conditions in the definition of a certain class of people. How many of us have not felt that differences in defining human life and human goals animate many of the conflicts in our society and in our world? How many of us have heard someone, perhaps ourselves, claim that truths are merely a matter of definition? It strains our imaginations to think about a world where definitions had no importance, and where people would be puzzled by a request for one. We probably feel that such a world would be confused and chaotic. How would you feel if, when you asked someone for a definition, that person replied

---

Euclid (350-275 B.C.) was a Greek mathematician who taught in Alexandra, Egypt. He is best known for his work *Elements* - the first complete mathematics text we possess.
Plato (C. 427-347 B.C.) was a Greek philosopher who was born and taught in Athens, Greece. Socrates' most important student, he wrote many philosophical dialogues and founded a school - The Academy.
Ludwig Wittgenstein (1889-1951) was born in Vienna, Austria and taught at Cambridge University, England. One of the creators of modern logic and 20th century philosophy, his major work is *Philosophical Investigations.*

that it didn't really matter? The difficulty we feel in comprehending such a response reveals how deeply Socrates' simple question and attitude infiltrates an entire structure of our society. It pervades how we understand language, knowledge, the subject matters we study, and even our sense of intellectual responsibility. Most of us have been embarrassed in the middle of an argument when we have been asked for the definition of a crucial term we were using and have been unable to respond adequately. Though we may well have felt we knew exactly what we were talking about, our failure probably shook our confidence. And nowhere is this feeling about the importance of definitions stronger than in mathematics.

Plato's student, Aristotle, spent great effort defining definition. This of course may seem paradoxical and circular. If definition itself needs to be defined, then it is not unlikely that thoughtful people have disagreed about it. In fact, this has happened. People have disagreed about the definition of definition, about why and when we need definitions, about what types of words can be defined, and how much we need to know previously about something in order to understand its definition. Some thinkers, following Socrates' presentation in the text you will read, have felt that the objects we call by the same name must have something in common that causes us to use the same word. The definition captures what is common to a group or class of things. For these thinkers, the task of definitions is to spell out how a certain type of thing is similar to certain other kinds of things and yet also different. To define humans as rational animals claims that humans are like other animals in certain ways and yet unique among animals in the fact that they have reason. To define humans as featherless bipeds accepts this definition of definition but offers a different account of our uniqueness. So, even if one accepts a certain claim about what a definition looks like in form, one can disagree about what its content should be.

One can also, however, disagree with the Socratic-Aristotelian attitude. Wittgenstein, in the second text, believes that things that we call by the same name – for example, "games" – have nothing specific in common. Rather, they display a variety of resemblances and overlapping traits which he compares to the similarities among family members. When considering this difference between Socrates and Wittgenstein, you might explore which better describes our attitude towards the definition of a straight line in mathematics. Do straight lines, for example, all share something in common, or are they similar to Wittgenstein's description of games? **(Now, read all the texts.)**

The third text for this lesson contains some of the definitions which Euclid uses for his geometry book, *Elements*, and some alternative definitions of a straight line. The *Elements* is one of the earliest mathematical works in which proofs of theorems are set out. Before he begins his systematic setting forth of geometrical proofs, Euclid states a number of definitions. These concern "point", "line", straight

13

line", and other geometrical terms. Since we are, to a certain extent, already familiar with these particular terms, one must wonder why he defines them. In addition, to say that we are already familiar with the terms Euclid defines also forces us to ask whether his definitions depend on our familiarity. In what way are the words he uses in his definitions of terms such as "line", "circle", "parallel", etc., related to our knowledge and experience? Are those definitions, such as *a line is breadthless length* or *a straight line is a line which lies evenly with the points on itself,* more general, or helpful in focusing our attention on something specific about points and lines, or do they have some other function? In other words, which of the words defined ("point", "line", "straight line", "circle", and "parallel") do you think he already expects you to know, or at least be familiar with, though perhaps not in the way he defines them? Which of them do you think you could learn entirely from his definitions?

Euclid never actually uses his definitions of the first four objects listed in this reading when he proves his theorems. Two questions naturally arise: Why then does he include them, and Where did he discover what they should contain? There are a number of possible directions for answering the latter question. It might be that he studied how we actually use these words and his definitions describe the most common and acceptable usage, just as if he were producing a dictionary. Or he might be highlighting certain aspects of our use of these words and removing other aspects in order to be precise. Or perhaps he had an insight into a special set of objects we don't usually experience and his definitions describe these objects to us. Or he might be making them up for the specific purpose of doing mathematics, which is entirely a construct of the human mind. We should consider each of these possibilities in turn.

Suppose some suggests that his definitions merely capture what we really mean when we use the words "line", "point", "straight line", "parallel", and "circle". However, a small child can use "circle" and "straight line" perfectly well, even to the point of correcting us if we purposely or accidentally misuse them. Yet that child probably would not understand Euclid's definitions of "straight line" or "circle". Why doesn't the child say, "Oh, that's what I always meant," when told that a straight line is a line that lies evenly with the points on itself? One could also suggest that Euclid's definitions are there in order for him to be more precise or exact compared to how we speak ordinarily. Sometimes we use "circle" for a regular round shape and "straight line" for the edge of a ruler, but in mathematics we must be more precise. We must use words exactly and consistently and therefore we must produce specific definitions. Or one might take a different approach and suggest that those definitions give us new information. We have probably previously thought of a point as a kind of dot or tiny spot, and that certainly has parts. Euclid's definition would be informing us that we were wrong. Contrary to our previous opinions, points do not have parts. If our

14

senses do not present such points to us, then Euclid is telling us that *this mathematics* concerns a realm of objects we have never experienced through sensation. The points we see have parts, but mathematics deals with points that have no parts, points we don't see but only think about. Or is Euclid pursuing a different path? Is the mathematician taking relatively ordinary words, such as "point", "line", "circle", "parallel", etc., and assigning those words new and special technical meanings? That is, is he creating his own definitions? But if he is assigning special technical meanings, why doesn't he just make up some new words instead of using familiar words which have a multitude of meanings and associations, such as "point" and "straight line"? Why not introduce two new terms, "hab" and "lek", and define them? *A hab is that which has no parts; a lek is breadthless length.* Euclid's third definition would become *the extremities of a lek are habs.* In short, what role do our previous opinions about points and lines play in relation to Euclid's definitions?

Finally, consider Euclid's definition of "straight line", and compare it with the definitions that some other mathematicians have given. These definitions are quite different. Euclid talks about points, Archimedes about comparative lengths, Leibniz about dividing a plane, and Lobachevski about positions in space and the result of the rotation of a surface. Each definition gives a very different perspective on a straight line and probably on what a definition should accomplish. Euclid considers the elements of a straight line to be points and asks how the line relates to them. Would you, from Euclid's definition, have a sense of what a straight line looks like, or do you need to know that in advance? Archimedes' definition, *a straight line is the shortest distance between two points,* says nothing about the parts of a straight line. Rather, it states how a straight line differs from other lines in regards to length. Is the fact that the straight line is the shortest distance between two points what you normally think of when you think of a straight line, or when you imagine a straight line, or is it something you discover later about straight lines? How would you argue that, though it appears to be a mere property of a straight line, this fact is really its central meaning? Another definition, similar to the Archimedean one that does not refer to length is, "A straight line is the one line between two points that is unique." Which of these two definitions would you prefer and why? Is it an advantage or disadvantage that no particular characteristic of the straight line is mentioned in this definition except in its uniqueness? The last two definitions in the text take us very far from what we usually think of about straight lines. The division of a plane or how a line is rotated seems very far from capturing either the linearity or straightness of a straight line. So the questions emerge: Why did these mathematicians choose these indirect approaches? What purpose might these definitions serve?

TEXTS

Plato: *Meno*

Socrates: What if someone asked you, "What is shape?" and you replied that roundness is shape. Wouldn't he then ask you as I did, "Do you mean it is shape or a shape?" And wouldn't you reply of course, that it is *a* shape.

Meno: Certainly.

Socrates: Your reason being that there are other shapes as well.

Meno: Yes.

Socrates: And if he went on to ask you what they were, you would tell him. Seeing that you call these many particular things by one and the same name, and that you say that every one of them is a shape, even though they are the contrary of each other, what is it that embraces round as well as straight? What do you mean by shape when you say that straightness is a shape as much as roundness? You do say that, don't you?

Meno: Yes.

Socrates: And in saying it, do you mean that roundness is no more round than it is straight, and straightness no more straight than round?

Meno: Of course not.

Socrates: Yet you do say that roundness is no more a shape than straightness, and the other way about.

Meno: Quite true.

Socrates: Then what is this thing called shape? Try to tell me. If when asked this question either about shape or color you said, "But I don't understand what you want, or what you mean," your questioner would perhaps be surprised and say, "Don't you see that I am looking for what is the same in all of them?" Would you be unable to reply, if the question was, "What is it that is common to roundness and straightness and the other things which you call shapes? "Do your best to answer.

Meno: No, you do it, Socrates.

TEXTS

Wittgenstein: *Philosophical Investigations*

Think about what we call "games". I mean board-games, card-games, ball-games, Olympic games and so on. What do they all have in common? Don't say, "There must be something they all have in common or they wouldn't all be called games." Rather, *look* and *see* whether there is, in fact, anything in common. If you do look at them you will not see something that is common to all of them. Instead, you will see similarities and relationships of various kinds. To repeat: don't think but look! We would see similarities crop up and then disappear. The result of this examination is: we see a complex network of similarities. They overlap, and crisscross. Sometimes there are large similarities, sometimes the similarities are in the details.

I can think of no better way to describe these similarities among games than as "family resemblances". The various resemblances among members of a family – the build, facial features, eye color, walk, attitude, and temperament – overlap and crisscross in the same way. So I shall say: "games" form a family.

Euclid: *Elements*
Definitions

1. A **point** is that which has no part.
2. A **line** is breadthless length.
3. The extremities of a line are points.
4. A **straight line** is a line that lies evenly with the points on itself.
5. A **circle** is a plane figure contained by one line such that all the straight lines falling upon it from one point among those lying within the figure are equal to one another.
6. **Parallel** straight lines are straight lines that, being in the same plane and being produced indefinitely in both directions, do not meet one another in either direction.

17

Alternative Straight Line Definitions

4a. Archimedes' definition: A straight line is the shortest distance between two points.

4b. Leibniz's definition: A straight line is one that divides a plane into two halves identical in all but position.

4c. Lobachevski's definition: A straight line fits upon itself in all its positions. (By this I mean that, during the revolution of the surface containing it, the straight line does not change its place if it goes through two unmoving points in the surface. That is, if we turn the surface containing it about two points of the line, the lines does not move.)

Questions

1. Below are listed five objects defined by Euclid. Check the boxes you feel characterize each of the Euclidean definitions.

	Informative	Useful	Clear	No Previous Knowledge Required
point				
line				
straight line				
circle				
parallel lines				

Informative means it tells you something new about the object.

Useful means you could use only the definition and not other knowledge whenever that word is used.

Clear means you do not feel you need to ask Euclid for further clarification.

No previous knowledge required means you would recognize what is defined purely from your knowledge of the words of the definition.

2. Compare the four definitions of "straight line". Decide which you think best and give a reason for your choice.

3. Look up the word "mathematics" in a dictionary. Which of the characteristics mentioned in #1 are satisfied by the definition? Which are not? Do you think the dictionary definition is informative, useful, etc?

4. Think of a word that could not be adequately defined. Why do you think that it cannot be defined?

II

DO WE CREATE NUMBERS?

TEXTS: Dedekind, *Continuity and Irrational Numbers, and The Nature and Meaning of Numbers.*

Orientation:

We all use numbers in our most ordinary activities. Counting numbers like 1,2,3,4,..., and fractions play a continual role in what we do. In weather reports or in the financial sections of newspapers, we often see negative numbers and zeros. In chemistry and physics classes, we run into rational numbers, and in algebra or other mathematics textbooks we confront imaginary numbers, the irrationals, and the real numbers. What are all these numbers that we talk about in different contexts? When we talk about tables, trees, emotions, thoughts, and music, we assume we refer to things that obviously exist. These objects are an essential part of the world we commonly experience. Tables and music are made by people, the former to be used in our homes, the latter to be enjoyed or reflected upon. Emotions and thoughts are an intimate aspect of human life and perhaps also of the lives of some non-human creatures. Trees are different from all these. They stand apart from us with a peculiar kind of independence, though, as we all know, we can enjoy them, write poems about them, rest under them, plant them, harvest them, create new kinds, and destroy them. Which of these kinds of things are numbers like?

Do numbers exist in the external world, or do they exist in our minds, or are they objects that we have made? Are they like trees, which we come upon in the world, or are they like thoughts and emotions, which somehow exist within us, or are they like tables or music, which are created by us, one to be a kind of tool we use in our lives, the other as an object of reflection or feeling? Or are they different from all of these? Do they exist in a slightly different realm that we don't see, but to which what we see or experience enables our thinking or imagination to have some kind of access? Dedekind, in this unit's texts, states his opinion with no hesitation. Numbers are created by human minds. They are tools!

Dedekind was a 19th century mathematician who confronted what he considered a serious defect in mathematics: its dependence on visual or mental images, drawings, and illustrations – in other words, its dependence on geometry and

Richard Dedekind (1831-1916) was born in Brunswick, Germany. He studied at Göttingen with the great mathematician Carl Gauss. He was appointed Professor of Mathematics first in Zürich and in 1862 at his home town of Brunswick. He led the movement to give rigorous definitions of basic mathematical concepts. He is best known for his studies on continuity, his definition of real numbers in terms of Dedekind's "cuts", and his definitions of infinite sets. His most famous work is *Continuity and Irrational Numbers.*

geometrical intuitions. He felt that when we use such geometrical diagrams we often think we understand more than we do. He feared that the drawing leads us to make assumptions we don't notice. To free arithmetic and algebra from geometry, however, he had to investigate a very troublesome type of number, the irrationals, – for example, √2 (the square root of 2), which we can only approximate by the infinitely long decimal 1.4142136... . The problems caused by the Pythagorean discovery of the √2 is what resulted in the 2500 year primacy of geometry over arithmetic as the foundation for all mathematics.

The √2 was discovered by the followers of Pythagoras, a Greek thinker who lived around 550 B.C. According to an ancient legend, the Pythagoreans swore their members to secrecy on this matter. The member who revealed it was, supposedly, later killed. At first glance, this is rather extreme for mathematicians, but the Pythagoreans thought of numbers as more than the elements of mathematics. The Pythagoreans believed that numbers were elements of whatever exists, a kind of building block of the universe. A simple example of this is, if we take a group of apples – say, two apples – and combine them with a group of three apples, we get a new group whose quantity is equal to the sum of the two numbers; that is, 2+3=5. These objects, apples, behave just like numbers. This was a startling insight. Truths about numbers could inform us about objects in the world. The Pythagoreans generalized this thought. They held that underlying and making possible the relations among objects in the world are the relations among numbers. Following this insight, they made many significant discoveries. For example, they first noticed the relation of musical harmonies, produced by differing lengths of wire or gut, to simple whole number ratios, like 1:2, and 1:3. This led them to believe that arithmetic was at the base of the order and harmony of the universe. This opinion was, however, quite fragile. If we construct a right triangle the length of whose sides are equal to 1, we get a hypotenuse whose numerical length is indeterminable. In other words, we cannot find a smaller line that will function as our unit of measurement, and that precisely measures both the sides and the hypotenuse of the triangle. The hypotenuse always remains unmeasurable. Since our unit of measurement represents the number 1, this means that there is neither a whole number nor a fraction which corresponds to the hypotenuse. The hypothenuse was built geometrically by using the sides of the triangle, but an arithmetical description of this construction does not exist. This discovery destroyed the Pythagoreans' understanding of the universe. For over 2000 years, arithmetic was replaced by geometry as the basis for mathematics.

In order to re-establish arithmetic as the foundation for all mathematics Dedekind must deal with the very issue that incapacitated the Pythagoreans: namely, the nature of √2. He must try to give an account of what this creature is; he must define and give an account of the irrational numbers. One way we come across the irrational numbers is when we try to perform the specific arithmetical operation of taking a square root of a certain number and fail. For example, the square root of 16 is 4, but there is no similar number which is the square root of 17. If there were such a number we would represent it as √17. This is the irrational number. Dedekind transforms this failure into the insight for understanding the nature of *all* numbers. The irrational number represented as the square root of 17 is created by us, we define it as the very number which when squared produces the number 17. Instead of numbers being the primary objects of arithmetic, as they were previously considered, he redefines all numbers as tools that are creations of the human mind and that are used to perform arithmetical operations. To make an analogy to our earlier example, *he reinterprets numbers:* they are less like trees and more like tables or hammers. So √2 becomes something like a tool, a human creation. What becomes primary for Dedekind is the cluster of arithmetical operations – counting, adding, subtracting, dividing, multiplying, and taking square roots. Numbers are tools that make possible a variety of human activities – for example, the activities of adding subtracting, dividing, etc. In this reading, we can see Dedekind's claim about how numbers are created as tools in relation to more familiar numbers such as integers and rationals.

Dedekind starts with the numbers created by the activity of counting. Counting is, he thinks, nothing other than the creation, one after another, of the series of numbers such as 1,2,3,4, and so on. This series does not end. It is infinite. With these numbers, two operations are always possible. If we add or multiply two counting numbers, the result is always another counting number, 4+4=8, and 4x4=16. The same is not true, however, for subtraction and division. If we subtract two counting numbers, sometimes we get a counting number and sometimes we don't. For example, 9–4=5, but 4–9 does not give us a counting number. This failure encourages a new creative act. We create a new type of number, which we call integers, in this case the negative integer -5, which equals 4–9. These new numbers make it possible to succeed whenever we subtract. We can now take any two integers, subtract one from the other, and get another integer as the answer. Sometimes the answer is a positive integer, as in (9–4) = +5, and sometimes it is a negative one, as in (4–9) = -5.

The new *system* of numbers, the integers, replaces the previous system, the counting numbers. The integers, like the counting numbers, can be added together to get another integer, but they can also, unlike the counting numbers, always be subtracted. For Dedekind, this new number system is a more powerful tool for the human mind. It is also a model of what he does with the other number systems he will create. The rational numbers are created for a similar reason. They ensure that division is always possible. Among counting numbers and integers, we can divide 4 by 2 and get another counting number, 2. But what about dividing 2 by 4? This does not give us either a counting number or an integer. We then create another number system, the rationals. Rationals are numbers of the form m/n, where m and n are both integers, e.g., $^5/_1$, $-^6/_3$. These numbers are such that the operations previously mentioned – addition, multiplication, and subtraction – hold for all of them. The rationals, however, also enable us to divide any two of them and get a result that is also a rational, except in the case of dividing by zero.[3] Dividing 2 by 4 becomes possible when these numbers are considered in their rational form. If we rewrite 2 and 4 as rational numbers, $^2/_1$ divided by $^4/_1$ gives us the rational $^2/_4$.

The simple example of subtraction, however, raises a number of issues. We have an intuitive sense of addition and subtraction among the counting numbers. Our intuitive sense is transformed, however, when we consider the integers. If we add two positive integers, we get a bigger integer. What happens when we add two negative integers? We get a "smaller" integer but a "bigger" negative integer. How about when we subtract two integers? Sometimes that's like "normal" subtracting, for example, in $(+9) - (+7) = +2$. But in a case like $(+9) - (-2) = +11$, it's like adding. The idea of what is normal has shifted dramatically. The fundamental difference and distinction between adding and subtracting is not as sharp as it was. So the more powerful tool isn't created without a certain cost, and this fact opens the way for a series of questions. Should we believe that *all* numbers are created or that only some kinds are? What is the nature of this creative act? How is it like or unlike other kinds of creative acts, like writing poetry, composing music, or building something? If Dedekind's idea of numbers as powerful tools contains a degree of arbitrariness, as the blurring of the distinction between addition and subtraction suggests, is that a reason for trying to base mathematics on geometry rather than arithmetic? Does the taint of arbitrariness permeate all mathematics? Many people report that they were good at mathematics when they were doing geometry, but had great difficulty with algebra, which is really a generalization of arithmetic. In geometry, many students are assisted by the very diagrams and images that Dedekind wishes to eliminate in order to bring out clearly and precisely what we assume. Is the cost worth the gain? However, couldn't we imagine someone getting very excited about what we have just called arbitrariness? Couldn't someone see this as a great advantage and a great discovery? We used to believe that addition and subtraction were very different. Now because of the creation of the system of integers – the positive and negative number system – we realize they are very similar, if not the same.

---

[3] You might want to discuss this special case. Should we leave division by zero undefined, or does it seem possible to argue that it really equals a specific number, or should we simply define it as equalling a specific number?

TEXTS

Dedekind: *Continuity and Irrational Numbers*

My attention was first directed toward the considerations that form the subject of this pamphlet in the autumn of 1858. As a professor in Zürich I found myself for the first time obliged to lecture upon the elements of higher mathematics, and felt more keenly than ever before the lack of a really scientific foundation for arithmetic. In presenting various theorems about continuity, I had recourse to geometric diagrams and examples. Now, as a teacher, I regard such a resort to geometric intuition in a first presentation of arithmetic, algebra, and calculus as exceedingly useful. It is indeed indispensable, if one does not wish to lose too much time. But no one will deny that this form of introduction can make no claim to being scientific. For myself this feeling of dissatisfaction was so overpowering that I made the fixed resolve to keep meditating on the question till I should find a purely arithmetic and perfectly rigorous foundation for the principles of mathematics.

Dedekind: *The Nature and Meaning of Numbers*

Numbers are free creations of the human mind. They enable us to grasp more easily and sharply the differences in things. If we study carefully what is done when we count a group of things, we notice the ability of the mind first to relate one thing to another, then to let one thing correspond to another, and finally to let one thing represent another. These are abilities without which no thinking is possible. It is on this indispensable foundation that the entire science of numbers must be established. From the time of our birth, we continually and increasingly are led to relate one thing to another and to let one thing stand for another. This is the power of our minds on which depends the creation of numbers.

Dedekind: *Continuity and Irrational Numbers*

I regard the whole of arithmetic as a necessary, or at least natural, consequence of the simplest arithmetic act, that of counting. Counting itself is nothing else than the successive creation of the infinite series of numbers, in which each new number is defined by the one immediately preceding it. The simplest act of counting is the passing from an already-formed individual number to the consecutive new one to be formed, i.e., from 4 to 5. The chain of these numbers forms in itself an exceedingly useful instrument for the human mind. It presents an inexhaustible wealth of remarkable laws obtained by the introduction of the four fundamental operations of arithmetic – addition, multiplication, subtraction, and division. Addition is the combination of any arbitrary repetition of the above-mentioned simplest act into a single act. Adding 2 + 4 means counting up to 2 and then counting 4 more from there. In a similar way, multiplication arises from counting. While the performance of these two operations, addition and multiplication, is always possible with counting numbers, the inverse operations, subtraction and division, prove to be limited.

Whatever the immediate occasion may have been, whatever comparisons or analogies with experience or intuition may have led to it, it is certainly true that just this limitation in performing the indirect operations of subtraction and division has in each case been the real motive for a new creative act. Thus negative and fractional numbers have been created by the human mind. In the system of all rational numbers, which results from these two creative acts, there has been gained a tool of infinitely greater perfection than we previously had. This system, which I shall name R (for rational number), possesses first of all a completeness and self-containedness that I consider would be a characteristic of a *body of numbers*. It consists in this: that the four fundamental operations are always performable with any two individuals in R, i.e., the result is always an individual of R, the single case of division by the number zero being excepted.

Let us take one more step and point out another property of the system R. I can express that property by saying that the system R the rational numbers forms a well-ordered domain of one dimension extending to infinity on two opposite sides. Now that description uses terms borrowed from geometric language, viz., the terms "dimension" and "sides". I will try, however, to translate this sentence into purely arithmetic properties in order to show how to avoid even the appearance that arithmetic stands in need of ideas foreign to it from geometry.

To express that the symbols a and b represent one and the same rational number we put $a=b$ as well as $b=a$. The fact that two rational numbers, a and b, are different is shown in this, that the difference $(a-b)$ has a positive or a negative value. If positive, then a is greater than b and b is less than a, (also represented by $a>b$, $b<a$). Whenever $(b-a)$ is positive – which is the same as $(a-b)$ is negative, then $b>a$, $a<b$. With regard to these two ways in which numbers may differ, the following laws will hold:

I. If $a>b$, and $b>c$, then $a>c$. (Geometrically, we might say b lies between a and c.)

II. If a and c are different numbers, then there are infinitely many different numbers between them.

III. If a is any specific number, then all numbers in R fall into two classes, A_1 and A_2. Each of the classes contains infinitely many members. The class A_1 comprises all numbers a which are less than a (we will call them a_1); the class A_2 comprises all numbers a_2 that are greater than a. The number a may be assigned to A_1 or A_2, as we will, it being the greatest of the class A_1 or the least of class A_2. In every case and circumstance, a separation or R into A_1 and A_2 results in every number of A_1 being less than every number of A_2.

These laws, though more complicated, allow us to state exactly what is meant by the geometrical description that the rational numbers form a well-ordered domain of one dimension extending to infinity on two opposite sides. In other words, this shows how arithmetic does not require a geometrical foundation to state its laws.

26

Questions

1. Suppose you are a career counselor and two people come to you for advice about whether they would be good at certain professions. All you know about them is that person A is much better at geometry than at algebra, the other, person B, is much better at algebra. Check which profession you would recommend to each. You may recommend the same profession to both.

	Person A (Better at Geometry)	Person B (Better at Algebra)
a) A newspaper reporter		
b) A basketball coach		
c) An actor		
d) A musician		
e) A surgeon		
f) An architect		
g) A politician		
h) An artist		

2. a) Do you find it easier to understand geometry or algebra?
   b) What do you feel causes problems for you in one or the other?
   c) Imagine that someone gave an answer different from yours. How is that person different from you?

3. State one way Dedekind's creative act of the human mind in mathematics is similar to writing poetry and one way it is different.

III

METAPHORS IN MATHEMATICS
TEXT: Galileo, *Two New Sciences*

Orientation:

In mathematics, as in other fields, metaphor and analogy play a significant role. Mathematics is no more cut-off from our everyday experience of the world than poetry, social sciences, or physics are, and mathematical concepts often emerge from concepts employed in other realms. A striking example is the word "geometry" itself. Once used to describe the activity of measuring land and parts of the earth, it was extended – perhaps initially as a metaphor – to designate the properties of triangles, rectangles, and circles, that made this measurement possible. Now, of course, no one would use the word "geometry" to describe the work of a surveyor or cartographer. The use of the terms "rational", "real", "irrational", and "roots" in reference to numbers also carry little or nothing of their original metaphorical use. This type of extension also happens within mathematics itself; concepts from one field of mathematics are often extended to others. Frequently, this happens metaphorically at first. Then the metaphor is carefully defined in the new situation, and eventually it takes on a life of its own. A case of this type is the concept of "curve" – once a geometrical concept and now also and principally an algebraic one. Another example is the concept "square", originally the name of a four sided figure and then also the name of a type of number. In no instance, however, has this issue of extending a concept been more dramatically visible than in regard to the finite and infinite.

The first issue concerning the infinite that confronts anyone is why the concept of the infinite is necessary at all. Everything we see in our daily lives is finite. No particular experience presents us with either the infinitely large or the infinitely small. Every collection of objects we confront has a definite number, and each has a specific size. This is true even if we cannot determine what that number or size is. Sometimes the number or size of things we experience is indefinite, but this probably does not lead any of us to expect that we could someday experience the infinitely large or small by improving the tools we use to count and measure. Whatever tools we use to extend our experience – microscopes, even of the most complex and sophisticated

---

Galileo (1564-1642) was born in Pisa, Italy. He became Professor of Mathematics at Padua, where he worked to improve the telescope as an astronomical instrument. He was one of the first to use this instrument to explore the skies. One of the creators of modern science, he employed mathematical descriptions of natural phenomena and proposed using experimentation. His two major works – *Two New Sciences* and *Concerning Two World Systems* - were both written in dialogue form. In 1633, he was summoned to Rome to face trial by the Inquisition for his views on the solar system. Forced to deny that the earth moved around the sun, he was sentenced to an enforced residence in Siena.

kind, or enormous space station telescopes – those instruments, though giving us access to the enormous or the minute, always give us finite values. Yet, in spite of this, the concepts of the infinite and infinitesimal seem to hover near our thinking. Just as we use a metaphor to extend a concept or image, we seem tempted to extend the concepts of size, number, distance, and time beyond the finite objects, quantities, spaces and durations we experience. We talk about the infinite size of the universe, the eternity of time, the infinitesimal size of a black hole. However, if our experience does not present the infinite and the infinitesimal to us directly, do these ideas emerge from mathematical, scientific, philosophical, or cosmological considerations?

In the ancient world, among the Greeks and Romans, few thinkers advocated the actual infinite, an infinite where all of the terms or members or parts are present at once. Those who did were, on the whole, thinkers who believed in the existence of atoms, for example, Lucretius and Empedocles. They argued that the universe and space must be endless because we cannot conceive a limit to them. Since they believed that all things are made up of atoms, they therefore had to explain how, in an endless universe, there could be enough atoms in any one place for larger compounds to form. Their explanation was that just as the universe is endless, so too the number of atoms must be infinite. Aristotle, however, is much more representative of ancient attitudes. He felt that the idea of an actual infinite is incoherent and paradoxical. In addition, he felt that the actual infinite plays no role in accounting for the objects we experience, nor in understanding space, motion, or time. Instead, faced with certain quantities that could be of any size or number, quantities without any intrinsic limit – e.g., a line of any length, or the number of its parts – he developed the concept of the potential infinite.

The potential infinite is an intermediate notion between the finite and the actual infinite. In fact, our use of the category of the potential infinite is somewhat similar to what we do when we speak metaphorically. A metaphor extends an idea into a new realm, but always with the sense that it is merely a temporary extension. A metaphor is something we create, not something we claim is literally in the world. The potential infinite is similar. When we speak of something as potentially infinite, we mean that it can always be bigger or more numerous, but it is never literally infinite. For Aristotle, lines, points, and moments of time are always finite. They require the action of a human being to make them larger or more numerous. For example, consider the division of a line into parts. We can divide any given line as often as we like. The number of parts into which it can be divided is potentially infinite, but the division of the line requires our action. The parts of a line are not in the line waiting and ready to be separated.

Starting in the 16-17th centuries, this attitude changes. Thinkers do not feel that the concept of the actual infinite is any less paradoxical or even less incompre-

-hensible than Aristotle did. However, they begin to hold that the infinite is essential for rendering an adequate account of the world and for doing mathematics. They, therefore, like Galileo in this text, struggle to develop a mathematical concept of the infinite that gives some content to our vague ideas, and avoids at least some of the worst paradoxes. They attempt to go beyond a metaphorical extension to create a literal use. They attempt to give the concept of the infinite a definite, permanent meaning. This also happens with ordinary words: words that have a single literal meaning are extended first by metaphor to new realms and then given specific meanings in those realms. "A blue table" is a literal use of the color word "blue". We can also, however, use this word metaphorically: someone might call a particular sound "blue". The word takes on a new and almost literal sense, however, when someone is in a blue mood, and is completely literal in the derivative expression "she sings the blues."

When we extend a concept from the finite to the infinite, we must make a series of decisions. Just as not all the characteristics of the color blue would apply to a mood or a certain type of music, so also not all the characteristics of finite numbers or lines are appropriate for our purposes. In other words, we must decide which common properties or operations would prove useful in dealing with the infinite. Can we imagine, or describe, or define characteristics or properties for the infinite analogous to those for finite quantities? If we think that it would be useful to state that two infinites are equal or unequal, can we transfer certain aspects of finite equality or inequality that would give some content to our claim? Other possible properties or operations might be "part and whole", "greater than", "less than", "as many as", "as much as", addition, subtraction, division, and multiplication. Each of these has a very definite sense when we are dealing with finite numbers. We must ask, first, whether it would be useful to extend any of these properties or operations to the realm of the infinite and, then, whether it is possible to do so, at first metaphorically, but finally in a more precise way.

In the accompanying text, Galileo confronts these issues in dialogue form in respect to one property: equality. Among finite numbers, if one number is greater than another, then we conclude that they are not equal. If $12 > 10$, then $12 \neq 10$. This is as obvious a truth as we can mention. Among the "infinite" collection of natural numbers (1,2,3,4,...) and the "infinite" collection of even numbers (2,4,6,...), however, we can show that there are more natural numbers than evens, since there are also the odds, and also that there are as many even numbers as there are natural numbers. This can be done by taking each natural number and doubling it. We always get a new even number. In other words, we can formulate a definite rule, doubling or multiplying by 2, such that we take each natural number, apply the rule, and get a unique even number which corresponds to it. This rule also enables us to claim that

30

every even number has been assigned to a unique natural number – the natural number that is equal to one half of it. So it appears we can show that there are *as many* even number as there are natural numbers.

Should we take another step, however, and ask *how many* natural numbers and *how many* even numbers there are? In other words, should we ask if the two groups are equal? If we decide to ask that question, and decide to create a way to answer it, should we use the criterion just sketched out to conclude that the "number" of natural numbers and the "number" of even numbers is the same number. At this stage, we have applied two points of view. By using one, we concluded that one group is greater than the other. Employing the other point of view, we concluded that there are *as many* members in one group as in the other. In contrast, among finite numbers, the claim that the number of natural numbers between 1 and 20 is greater than the number of even numbers between 1 and 20 is also the same as saying that there are not as many in the second group as in the first. Should we decide, because of this identity among finite numbers, that one cannot literally talk about "equal" and "greater than" in regard to the infinite? If so, we would have decided that we can only speak metaphorically about the infinite. However, there is another option. We could decide to break the equivalence between the two ways of looking at equality and inequality among finite quantities. We could decide that the difference between these two perspectives in determining quantity is exactly how we know we have an actual infinite instead of a finite quantity. In other words, the indication of the presence of the infinite is that one aspect of it – the evens – is a part of the other – the natural numbers – and also that there are *as many* even numbers as natural numbers. Galileo decides the first way, most modern mathematicians choose the second option.

Many claim that we are dealing with an actual infinite when the whole is both greater than some part and yet the elements of the part are as many as the elements of the whole. In our example, there are more natural numbers than evens, and there are as many even numbers as natural numbers. This approach would claim that we therefore have an actual infinite and that the "number" of the part is equal to the "number" of the whole. Remember that, in considering these issues, we are acting more like poets than scientists. We are taking concepts we know and that have specific relations to one another and modifying them, sometimes very drastically. The overriding question is, what are the advantages and disadvantages of these decisions? A comparable question is, what makes us decide that a merely metaphorical use of a word is so fertile and suggestive that we begin to create a new literal use for it?

31

TEXT

Galileo: *Two New Sciences*
(a dialogue among Simplicio, Salviati, and Sagredo)

Simplicio: We certainly find lines which differ in length. So if each line contained infinitely many points, the infinitude of points in the greater line would exceed the infinitude of points in the shorter line. The existence of an infinite greater than the infinite seems to me to be incomprehensible.

Salviati: These are some of the difficulties that emerge when we reason about infinities with our finite minds and apply to them those attributes that we usually apply to finite and bounded things. This, I think, is inconsistent. I don't think the attributes of "greater than", "less than", or "equal to" suit infinites. One can't say that one infinite is greater than, less than, or equal to another. To prove this, I'll share with you an argument that once occurred to me. I assume you know which numbers are squares and which are not squares.

Simplicio: Of course I know. A square number comes from multiplying a number by itself. 4 and 9 are squares, the first arising from 2 times itself, the second from 3.

Salviati: Good. And just as these products are called squares, those numbers that we multiply by themselves are called roots. And other numbers that don't arise from numbers multiplied by themselves are not squares. So I say that all numbers including squares and non-squares are more numerous than the squares alone. If I claimed that, you would agree wouldn't you?

Simplicio: Certainly.

Salviati: Next, if I ask how many squares there are, wouldn't it be right to say that there are as many squares as their own roots? This is because every square has its root, and every root has its corresponding square. In addition, no square has more than one number as its root, nor is any number the root of more than one square.

Simplicio: Exactly.

Salviati: So, if I ask how many roots there are, one couldn't deny that these are as numerous as all the numbers, since there is no number that isn't the root of some square. Since that is so, we must admit that square numbers are as numerous as all numbers. This is because there are as many squares as roots, and all numbers are roots. Yet, we claimed originally that there were many more numbers than squares. Indeed, the number of squares diminishes as one moves on to greater numbers. There are ten squares between 1 and 100, so 1/10th of the total numbers are squares. However, between 1 and 10,000 only 100 numbers are squares so 1/100th of the numbers are squares. Between 1 and 1,000,000 there are 1000 squares. This reduces the fraction to 1/1000th. Yet in the infinite number, if it is conceivable, there are as many squares as there are numbers.

Sagredo: Well, then, what shall we decide about this?

Salviati: I don't see that we have any alternative. We must admit that there are infinitely many numbers, infinitely many squares, and infinitely many roots. In addition, the number of squares is not less than that of all numbers, nor is the latter greater than the former. However, though we admit all this, we also claim that the attributes of equal, greater, and less have no place in describing infinite, but only finite qualities. So what do I say when Simplicio shows me several unequal lines and asks why there aren't more points in the greater? I reply that there are neither more, nor less, nor as many, but in each there are infinitely many.

Sagredo: Wait a moment. Let me add a thought which has just struck me. As things stand up to this point, we have decided that it is improper to claim that one infinite is larger than another. However, it seems to me that the infinite is not ever greater than the finite. For suppose the infinite number is greater than 1,000,000. It would follow that in passing beyond 1,000,000 to other larger numbers, one would be traveling toward the infinite. But this isn't so. In fact, the opposite seems to be more plausible: that as we reach larger numbers, we get farther from the infinite. For with numbers, the larger they get, the scarcer become the squares contained within them. In the infinite number, however, there are as many squares as numbers. So to move toward larger numbers, according to this characteristic, moves you away from the infinite number.

Salviati: So by your ingenious reasoning, we conclude that the attributes of greater, equal, and less are out of place not only between infinites, but between the infinite and the finite. If we continue your thought and your analogy, we reach an even stranger conclusion. It should follow that since going to larger numbers takes

33

us away from the infinite, reversing our direction should take us closer to it. In other words, if any number should be called infinite, it is unity. And truly in unity we find some of the characteristics we discovered about the infinite. In unity, there are as many squares as numbers, and as many cubes, fourth powers and others. So if any number qualifies as the infinite number, it is unity. These are some of the wonders that go beyond the bounds of our imagination. They warn us how seriously one errs in trying to reason about infinites by using the same attributes we apply to the finite. For the natures of these have no necessary relation between them.

Questions

1. Listed below are 12 uses of the word "sharp". The literal meaning of "sharp" appears in the sentence "The knife has a sharp edge." For each use on this list decide on a word or phrase you could substitute for "sharp". Then decide whether the use there is metaphoric or literal. The different literal uses should be described as L_1, L_2, etc.

   1) A has a sharp tongue.
   2) B has a sharp mind.
   3) C has a sharp wit.
   4) D is a sharp dresser.
   5) E looks sharp.
   6) F is sharp.
   7) G came at 12 o'clock sharp.
   8) H felt a sharp desire for food.
   9) I played an A sharp on the piano.
   10) J keeps a sharp watch on things.
   11) K gave very sharp criticism.
   12) L is a sharp contrast to O.

2. Where do you think you got the idea of the infinite?

3. Which of the following properties do you feel would be helpful in describing the infinite, if you were speaking *metaphorically?*
   a) equality   b) part and whole   c) greater than
   d) less than   e) as many as   f) other

   Now, answer this same question again, but assume you are speaking *literally*.
   a) equality   b) part and whole   c) greater than
   d) less than   e) as many as   f) other

   Choose any *one* of your responses to question #3, and give a reason for your decision.

IV ARE ONLY SOME PEOPLE GOOD AT MATH?
TEXT: Pascal, *Pensées*

Orientation:

Most of us don't remember what we were like in the 2nd or 3rd. grade. Were we good at math or weren't we? How about in the 6th or 7th grades? Do we remember what we were like at that age? What do you think 3rd and 7th graders would say about themselves if they were asked, "Are you good at math?" Studies show that most third graders and almost 75% of 7th graders think that they are good at mathematics. However, studies also show that when randomly chosen 9th or 10th graders are asked that same question, only about 20% will answer positively. What has happened? Were nearly all eight year olds good at math, though only 20% of all 15 and 16 year olds are still good at it? What happened to the other 80%? Were the 3rd graders right or wrong? Another possibility is that only 20% were really good at it and the others only realized that by the time they were in high school. However, it may be that all 9th and 10th graders are good at it but most of them don't realize it because they aren't doing well in their mathematics courses. The question this series of questions leads to is: What does it mean to be good at math?

All of you have probably been confronted by a version of this question. Though few of you will choose to become professional mathematicians, all of you have demonstrated some skill and ability in mathematics, even if you find yourselves afraid of it. Most of you have probably been asked either *why* you like mathematics or how it is you're able to get "that stuff". These questions look much simpler than they are. They look as though they are merely requesting a report or a description of a fact about you. They are, however, really much more complex. Such a question is usually not asked merely as a point of information. The people who ask are puzzled about you and about themselves. Whether those who ask are friends, parents, or other students, they probably ask because they have concluded that they lack certain abilities that you appear to have. They are therefore really asking, "How are you different from me?" When you are confronted with this question, it is probably surrounded with layers of emotion and confusion.

In our society, the opinion that only certain people are good at mathematics

---

Blaise Pascal(1623-62) was born in Clermont-Ferrand, France. Pascal explored various topics in mathematics such as number theory and conic sections. He was also one of the first to investigate probability. In 1647, he invented a calculating machine. Later he worked on perfecting the barometer, the hydraulic press, and the syringe. His work in physics focused on the nature of fluids. A mystical experience converted him to a Catholic sect known as the Jansenists. His most famous work, *Pensées*, was published in 1669 after his death.

has tremendous consequences. One obvious consequence is that only relatively few students are encouraged to take mathematics courses all through high school, and this decision can play a crucial role in how they will spend their later working lives. In addition, the two groups of students think differently about themselves. "Getting math" is something admired; "not getting it" is a kind of embarrassment, if not worse. This does not mean that those who "get it" are admired because they will become mathematicians. Rather, they are admired because it is held that "getting math" makes it more likely that they will succeed at other tasks that are in fact highly esteemed. It is widely believed that ability in mathematics involves a kind of thinking, or a sort of intelligence, that makes possible the accomplishment of many tasks and goals that are not in any obvious sense mathematical. And that is not all: often, those who are held to be good at mathematics are considered "smart" and the others aren't. You can easily imagine, and probably have seen, the effect of such a claim. The self-respect, motivation, and the possibility of accomplishing certain goals vanishes for many students. This not only has serious educational effects, but also deep economic, political, and social consequences. Students carry the scars of this apparently straight-forward claim far into their adult life.

There was a period in your schooling when these labels were not yet applied. It is roughly in middle school that the groups begin to divide. It is not clear, however, why this happens. It may be that the current methods of teaching mathematics appeal only to a certain kind of student. It may have nothing to do with a student's ability, but only with how the subject is approached. Some have argued for this by pointing out that some of the more thoughtful students are the ones who have the most difficulty. You probably all remember someone in a math class asking a question such as, "Why is $2^0 = 1$?" and being told, "It's just that way." Or hearing that same unhelpful answer when a student wondered aloud why the product of two negative numbers is positive. This type of situation happens all the time in mathematics classes in middle school and in high school. We can understand that a very thoughtful student could get very troubled by these responses and begin to believe that he or she just can't get it. This becomes a self-fulfilling prophecy.

The text by Pascal deals explicitly with some of these issues and focuses our consideration on other issues by supplying some concepts that we can either accept or modify. He distinguishes and describes two types of minds. He calls them the mathematical and the intuitive. For him, these minds occupy the two ends of the intellectual spectrum. They seem radically different from one another, and each has a very definite strength as well as a defect. In fact, the strength and weakness seem to go together. The mathematical mind is capable of understanding principles or axioms about objects it has never experienced in daily life. Such a mind can turn its attention to perfect triangles and absolutely straight lines, to irrational and imaginary numbers, and to infinite sets. It can grasp the principles that underlie these, and draw correct conclusions. The intuitive mind, in contrast, does not seem to reason actively at all. An intuitive mind thinks without steps. Such thinking is almost like feeling. Such a person could walk into a room filled with strangers, size up the situation at a glance without any need to figure it out, and do and say just what is called for. Each of these abilities, however, comes along with a corresponding defect. The mathematical mind tries to approach life by means of axioms and theorems, and so, at times, becomes ridiculous. The intuitive mind can't free itself from the particular details of its experience in order to grasp more general and abstract truths. **(Now, read the texts.)**

Does Pascal's description ring true to you as characterizing what it is like to be good at mathematics? If it doesn't, how do you think it should be modified? What aspects has he overlooked either about being good at mathematics, or not being able to "get it", and does he adequately explain why some people are afraid of mathematics? Pascal does not exclude the possibility that some minds are both mathematical and intuitive. This would be like having the best of both worlds. Such a person would be exceptionally able at the most abstract and general ideas and arguments, and yet also unusually savvy about people, politics, emotions, feelings, and whatever else we deal with in our everyday lives. Does your experience bear out this possibility? If such people are possible, do they alternate between being mathematical and intuitive at different stages in their life? Or do they switch from one to the other according to circumstance? If they do switch, is it the mathematical or intuitive aspect of the mind that knows when to switch gears? This issue is important even if one disagrees with Pascal's descriptions of these types of minds. For it may be that however one describes mathematical ability, it always comes with a cost. For example, in mathematics, one often has complete certainty about answers, truths, and proofs. Is it that people who are good at mathematics also have the characteristic of needing and expecting certainty in all things? Such people would have great difficulty in situations where there is not complete certainty, and increased difficulty as the uncertainty becomes greater. So the question we might ask is whether the same person who strives for certainty – for being right – can learn to handle uncertainty without trying to impose certainty on it. More generally, does ability in mathematics come with a cost and can it be corrected?

TEXTS

Pascal: *How mathematical and intuitive minds differ*

The principles the mathematical mind grasps are obvious. However, they are not the ones we daily and ordinarily use. So, because of our longstanding habits, it is very hard to turn our minds in that direction. However, once we do direct our attention to them, ever so little, we understand the principles fully. And then one's mind must be very careless to reason incorrectly from principles so plain that it is almost impossible not to grasp them.

The intuitive mind finds its principles in common daily experience. They are, in fact, in front of everyone. One has only to look, and no effort is required. One only needs good eyesight, but it must be very sharp. For the principles are so subtle and numerous that it is almost impossible that we see all of them. And if we miss one principle, we will make mistakes. So one must have exceptional sight to see all the principles and then an accurate mind not to reach false conclusions from them.

All mathematicians would be intuitive if they had sharp vision. For they reason accurately from principles they know. On the other hand, intuitive minds would be mathematical if they turned their eyes toward the very general mathematical principles they don't confront in their daily activities. The reason that some intuitive minds are not mathematical is that they can't turn their attention to the principles of mathematics. But the reason mathematicians are not intuitive is that they don't see what's in front of them.

Mathematicians are accustomed to very exact and simple principles. They don't reason well until they have carefully inspected and arranged them. They are therefore lost in matters of intuition, where the principles cannot be ordered. In fact, these principles are scarcely seen. It is more accurate to say we feel them rather than see them. And it's almost impossible to get those who don't feel the principles themselves to notice them. These principles are so fine and so numerous that your senses must be very delicate and clear to grasp them. And then drawing a conclusion from them is even harder because these conclusions can't be exactly demonstrated or proven as in mathematics. This is because these principles aren't known to us in the same way and because the proofs would be infinite. We must seize the conclusions at once, in one glance, and not primarily by a process of reasoning.

So it's very rare to find a mathematician who is intuitive, or an intuitive mind that is mathematical. Mathematicians make themselves ridiculous because they want

39

to treat matters of intuition mathematically. They want to begin with definitions and axioms, but such a procedure is completely inappropriate when applied to our daily experiences and activities. It isn't that the mind doesn't do this, but it does it naturally and immediately, and without any technical rules of reasoning. The description of this sort of reasoning is beyond all of us, and only a few can feel it.

Intuitive minds, on the other hand, judge at a single glance. They are therefore astonished when they are presented with mathematical propositions and theorems that they don't understand. In addition, when they are told that these theorems can only be approached through definitions and axioms which seem to them sterile and unnecessarily detailed, they are repelled and disheartened.

But dull minds are neither intuitive nor mathematical. Mathematicians who are only mathematical have exact minds as long as everything is explained to them by means of definitions and axioms. Otherwise they are inaccurate and insufferable. They are only right when the principles are entirely clear. And intuitive minds that are only intuitive don't have the patience to reach the very first principles of things. They therefore can't grasp the foundations of purely speculative and conceptual matters, which they have never seen in the world and which are beyond their daily experience.

Pascal: *On what people are*

No one is recognized in the world as skilled at poetry unless they have put up a sign announcing themselves as a poet. No one is recognized as good at mathematics unless they declare themselves to be mathematicians. But people who have really been educated don't want signs and labels. Educated people are not poets or mathematicians. They are all these, and judges of all these. No one guesses what they are. When they come into a group, they participate in whatever is being discussed. You don't notice one ability or skill in them rather than another, except when they have to use it. But then we notice it. It is typical of such people that we don't call them fine speakers, when giving a speech is not at issue. But when it is, we say they are fine speakers. It is a very false kind of praise to describe someone as a clever poet when they enter a room. But it is a very bad sign when someone is not called upon to give an opinion and judge a poem.

Questions

1. Arrange the group below as more or less similar on the two diagrams. On the straight line, place them as you feel they are more or less similar to P (poets) and M (mathematicians) which are put at extremes. In the circle you should decide how to position all of the items in respect to M (mathematicians). You are free to place any category you feel is appropriate across the diameter from M and arrange the others accordingly.

Poets (P)
Mathematicians (M)
Lawyers (L)
Doctors (D)
Composers (C)
Historians (H)
Engineers (E)

P _____ M

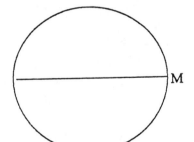

2. Which diagram in question #1 is a more accurate picture of human skills? Why?

3. Why are some people afraid of mathematics?

V STARTING TO THINK MATHEMATICALLY
TEXT: Euclid, *Elements*

Orientation:

Our mathematics has ancient sources: arithmetic, geometry, and the rudiments of algebra can be found in the civilizations of the Middle East – for example, Babylon, Ur and, of course, in Egypt. Much speculation has surrounded the origin of these human activities, since many thinkers have considered these discoveries as fundamental, decisive moments in the history of human beings. We hear a great deal in the media about how computers and other hi-tech innovations have changed our society. From our contemporary perspective, these tools do indeed appear to have drastically altered the way we live our lives. Much of what we used to do laboriously can now be accomplished more easily and faster. But the change from pre-computer to post-computer is a minute step compared to the chasm that we crossed when we somehow acquired the skill of counting and measuring objects. A people without the ready use of the rudiments of such knowledge would almost appear to us as another species. In the play, *Prometheus Bound,* written by Aeschylus in approximately 465 B.C., this Greek dramatist tries to imagine such a monumental moment. Prometheus, according to legend, stole fire from the gods and gave it and other gifts to man. In this play, Prometheus states that before his gifts "they looked, but didn't see; they heard, but didn't understand. Like shapes in a dream, they lived their lives in confusion." Later he declares about his gifts, "I invented numbers for mankind's use, the greatest of all gifts."

The great commercial and agricultural centers of the Middle East and Northern Africa supply us with records of specific arithmetical and geometrical rules used in the planning and building projects of complex societies. Legend has it that some of these rules were brought to Greece by Thales. This set the stage for the next great step, which rivals, as some claim, the gift of Prometheus in the significance of its consequences for how we live. During a period of a few hundred years in Greece, there is evidence that an entirely new attitude towards these practical rules emerged. That attitude, which we see first fully worked out by Euclid, is that arithmetic and geometry are not primarily a set of practical rules we discover in our daily activities,

---

Euclid (C. 350-277) B.C.) was a Greek mathematician who taught at Alexandria in Egypt, a great center of learning in the ancient world. Best known for his great work on geometry, *Elements*, he also wrote on conic sections, astronomy, optics, and music. Many philosophers and mathematicians have held that Euclid's *Elements* is one of the most influential works ever written in both its content and in presenting a model of thinking.

42

and which assist us in accomplishing countless tasks. Rather these rules are capable of being proven and demonstrated from a small set of basic claims assumed or believed to be true. A reader of Euclid's *Elements* is taken through a series of propositions, each of which contains a conclusion logically derived from premises. In short, what was a mere collection of rules became inter-related, demonstrated, and available to any reasonable human being. Thus came into existence a separate subject matter with a realm of its own - geometry - which was no longer merely a tool for measuring land and earth (hence its name) but now the very centerpiece of mathematics.

This new attitude changes the very nature of the way we think about ourselves. Many claim that it creates a division in our beliefs between those we claim to know and those we consider mere opinions. Knowledge, according to some thinkers, is what can be demonstrated and proved as in mathematics. What can't be proved is mere opinion. Mathematics, since the time of the Greeks, has been a principal example of knowledge – of what can genuinely be learned – and the goal towards which many other sciences strive. In fact, the word "mathematics" comes from *mathema*, the ancient Greek word that means "what is truly learned". It is therefore important both for our understanding of mathematics and for our understanding of ourselves to explore demonstration and proof at the moment they came into existence.

Often we try to prove things to one another. Generally, in order to succeed, we must be familiar with the person we are trying to convince. About politics, for example, a proof that convinces one person may not convince another. In mathematics, the situation is different. Mathematicians do not care whether they know anything about the listener or reader of a mathematical proof in order for it to succeed. It is only necessary that the reader understand the symbolic or technical language in which it is presented. Mathematical proofs are not intended for only some people, but rather for all people, whoever they are, whatever their experience. The moods, emotions, and attitudes of readers are not taken into account when a mathematical proof is at issue. The proof is either valid or invalid. If we, as readers, cannot follow a valid proof, it is our own fault.

Some proofs depend on previous proofs for the premises used to reach a new conclusion. But this dependence on previous proofs cannot recede infinitely. At some stage there must be a first proof whose premises are not the result of a previous proof. If this were not the case, the sequence of proofs would continue to regress. Nothing would support the whole structure. At some stage there must be a first proof. The questions we will consider in this lesson are: (1) How do we establish this first proof? (2) What does it mean to be convinced by a proof? First, of course, we need to ask what a demonstration or a proof is. Generally speaking, a proof attempts logically to demonstrate a conclusion. Statements that require demonstration are called *propositions* by Euclid. Some writers call them *theorems*. Ultimately, such demonstrations depend on other statements that we do not demonstrate. Euclid calls these *postulates*. Another name for them is *axioms*. But, what distinguishes a postulate from a proposition? There are a number of approaches to answering this question.

One might claim that one simply must start somewhere. Mathematicians who advocate this approach hold that propositions and postulates are really identical in type. We, as mathematicians, choose the ones to start with and the ones to demonstrate. There may be a number of reasons motivating our decision, but according to this approach none of these reasons implies that certain mathematical statements do not, in their nature, require demonstrations or proof and that others do. So we must locate something that is not merely arbitrary on which to base our choice as to what we will accept as a postulate and what we will demonstrate as propositions.

Other mathematicians take a different approach. They claim that postulates are more basic than propositions. Postulates make statements about the simplest objects in mathematics. Just as these simple objects – points and lines in the case of geometry – are used to build more complex objects – triangles and other figures – so the statements that describe them are used to build propositions describing the complex objects. This approach views the relation as similar to that between atoms and molecules.

Yet another approach claims that postulates do in fact differ radically from propositions. Postulates, advocates of this approach say, don't require demonstration, either because anyone who understands what postulates say grasps their truth, or because they contain within themselves their own demonstrations. This is usually stated as the claim that they are self-evident, that they carry their evidence along with them. On this view propositions differ from postulates either because recognizing the truth of propositions requires more than simply understanding the words, or because they do not carry with them the evidence of their truth. On this view, propositions differ from postulates either because only some people recognize their truth or because propositions don't contain their own demonstrations.

Euclid states five postulates at the beginning of his work. Superficially, they do not seem to be similar. The first four are short and grammatically simple. The last one is not. It is long and complicated. The first three state that something can be done: we can draw a line, extend it, and draw a circle with any radius. The last two make claims about geometrical objects: one asserts that all right angles are equal, the last one states the conditions when two lines meet. Yet in spite of these differences, Euclid considers all of these statements postulates. **(Turn to the text and read the**

postulates now. Don't read the proposition yet.)

What features do they all share, if any, that qualify them to come first and to be used to demonstrate propositions? Do they seem obviously true or conceptually simple? The next issue is their order. Are they five completely separate statements, or is there some order to them? One way to consider this question would be to explore reordering them. Could postulate #2 come before postulate #1? Could postulate #4 be stated before postulate #3? What would the postulates assume if we learned that straight lines can be extended before being told that a straight line can be produced from any point to any other point? Imagine you are a mathematician who proposes this new ordering of postulates #1 and #2. How would you justify your procedure? What would you have to claim about straight lines and points so that it would be reasonable to claim that one could extend an already existing straight line without having to know that between any two points a straight line can be drawn?

Whatever it is that establishes Euclid's order, it cannot be that some postulates are used to demonstrate others. None are demonstrated. So if there is an order, the later ones depend on the preceding ones in a way which differs from how propositions depend on previous postulates. This is particularly puzzling in regard to the fifth postulate. This postulate is long and very complex. In fact, we included a diagram in the text so that the statement could be followed more easily. Because Euclid chose to make this a postulate, one might assume that, in spite of its apparent complexity, it is fundamentally similar to the others. Can you detect a similarity? Some mathematicians have thought it should be a proposition and tried to prove it from the other four postulates. Euclid does not give any additional explanation for this approach. We can only assume that he believed the motive or justification for his approach would be self-evident to the reader, though up to now what this justification is has not been recognized. In the questions below, you are asked to give some account that makes Euclid's ordering of the postulates plausible.

After stating the postulates, Euclid presents and demonstrates the first proposition. This proposition does not describe or state a geometrical fact, though many propositions do. Some propositions describe the conditions under which triangles are congruent, others demonstrate claims about angle sums in figures, still others show how to construct figures. The first proposition demonstrates the construction of a geometrical figure, a special sort of triangle that has all of its sides equal. **(Turn to the text, re-read the postulates, and continue with proposition #1.)**

Is there any way we could have predicted or expected that this proposition would be first, or does this just happen to be the first one? When you create a plausible account to explain the order of the postulates, you might try to use the construction of the triangle as the culmination of a plausible sequence. The demonstration of the proposition uses some postulates explicitly. It also refers to the definition of the circle as a figure in which all lines drawn from the center to the circumference are equal, that is, all radii are equal. Does Euclid's demonstration convince you? The demonstration has an accompanying drawing. Was the drawing only helpful, or was it essential? If there were no drawing, would it have been harder to follow the demonstration or impossible to do so? Was there anything you gained from the drawing that should have been stated explicitly as a postulate? Most of you probably felt the demonstration was successful. Imagine someone who didn't feel that the construction was demonstrated. Was there a particular step you feel would have caused the problem? If you were trying to convince this person, would you go over Euclid's demonstration more carefully, or would you want an additional postulate to clear up the problem?

TEXT

Euclid: *Elements: Five Postulates and Proposition #1*

Postulates

Let the following be postulated:

1. It is possible to draw a straight line from any point to any point.
2. It is possible to produce a finite straight line continuously in a straight line.
3. It is possible to describe a circle with any center and distance.
4. All right angles are equal to one another.
5. If a straight line falling on two straight lines makes the interior angles on the same side less than two right angles, then the two straight lines, if produced indefinitely, meet on the side on which the angles are less than two right angles.

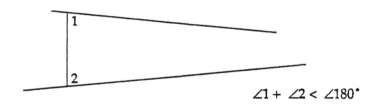

$$\angle 1 + \angle 2 < \angle 180°$$

Proposition #1.

    On a given finite straight line to construct an equilateral triangle.

Let AB be the given finite straight line.

Thus it is required to construct an equilateral triangle on the straight line AB.

With Center A and distance AB let the circle BCD be described.

Again, with center B and distance BA let the circle ACD be described. From the point C, in which the circles cut one another, to the points A,B, let the straight lines CA, CB be joined.

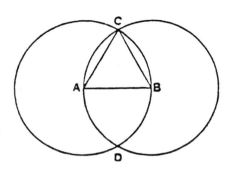

Now, since the point A is the center of the circle CDB, AC is equal to AB.

47

Again, since the point B is the center of the circle CAD, BC is equal to BA.

But CA was also proved equal to AB; therefore each of the straight lines CA, CB is equal to AB.

And things which are equal to the same thing are also equal to one another; therefore CA is also equal to CB.

Therefore the three straight lines CA, AB, BC are equal to one another.

Therefore the triangle ABC is equilateral; and it has been constructed on the given finite straight line, AB.

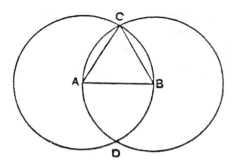

Questions

1. Choose among the three possibilities for each postulate. You may choose more than one category if you wish.

Postulates
1. It is possible to draw a straight line from any point to any point.
2. It is possible to produce a finite straight line continuously in a straight line.
3. It is possible to describe a circle with any center and distance.
4. All right angles are equal to one another.
5. If a straight line falling on two straight lines makes the interior angles on the same side less than two right angles, then the two straight lines, if produced indefinitely, meet on the side on which the angles are less than two right angles.

	Self-evident	More fundamental than a proposition	Just chosen by Euclid to get started
Postulate 1			
Postulate 2			
Postulate 3			
Postulate 4			
Postulate 5			

2. Create an account that makes sense of the order of the postulates. You should do this either by considering only the five postulates by themselves, or by the way they lead to the first proposition.

3. Is the diagram used in proposition #1 *necessary* for the proof or simply *useful*? If *necessary*, what could not be done without it? If *useful*, how does it help?

49

VI DEMONSTRATING THE UNPROVABLE
TEXT: Aristotle, *Metaphysics*

Orientation:

From the time Aristotle first articulated and described logic, this subject matter has engaged and fascinated many thinkers both in its own right and in relation to mathematics. Logic pervades the presentation of mathematical theorems because it forms the very structure of proofs and demonstrations. Some mathematicians and logicians have even held that mathematics and logic are not two different subject matters, that mathematics is really a branch of logic, or reducible to logic. Certain important characteristics of mathematics, such as the certainty of our conclusions and its independence of experience, also differentiate mathematics classes from other classes in the curriculum. Unlike science classes, mathematics classes have no laboratory experiments; unlike social studies classes, there are no historical facts. Unlike English classes, where interpretations of poems can be said to be better or worse, in mathematics classes we seem to possess certainty about right or wrong answers. These traits are similar to those of logic, and they are the reasons why many have viewed logic and mathematics as one subject. It is therefore important for us to explore the status of logic.

Logic is not something people notice in the normal course of speaking, writing, and thinking. In this, it is like grammar, which can serve as an example. Most people who speak and understand a language have little knowledge of grammatical forms. They know when a sentence makes sense and when a string of words is meaningless, even if they cannot describe the words as nouns, adjectives, clauses, and phrases. Many people, in fact, first learn grammar when they study a foreign language. Learning a foreign language can give the kind of distance necessary to notice how words differ and how they fit together. Do we need a similar distance to notice logical structure? What would it take to give us the distance from ourselves we might need to recognize that we are logical?

Let's see how it is when we confront a specific example of logic. We often present arguments and proofs to one another and become convinced, without ever noticing that when these are logical we often find them especially persuasive or undeniable. If we, for example, agree that "Socrates is a human being," and that "all

---

Aristotle (384-322 B.C.) was born in Stagera, Macedonia. In 366 B.C., he went to Athens to study with Plato. After Plato's death, he returned to Macedonia, where he was responsible for the education of Alexander the Great. He returned to Athens in 335 B.C. and formed a school of his own, the Lyceum. His writings include works on physics, metaphysics, politics, ethics, poetry, and biology. Aristotle's works have had as much influence on Western thought as those of any other writer.

human beings are mortal," then all of us would agree that "Socrates is mortal." This seems so obvious to us that we would hardly ever think about *how* it follows, about *why* the conclusion is inevitable. Yet here we are following a set of logical rules that hold in all other cases that have a similar form.

The issue is even more dramatic in relation to more basic logical principles. Who would bother even to state that "this tree is this tree" or "this object here can't be both a tree and not a tree"? The former is called the law of identity; the latter, the law of non-contradiction. In the case of these logical principles, we must look for a way in which the logical relations that we normally take for granted, and which are virtually invisible, can be brought forward and examined.

Once logic is discovered, we must ask what it is. There are roughly three possibilities:

First, there is the view that logic is the most general truth about all things – trees, animals, stones, triangles, numbers, and thoughts. It is the most basic and general way in which things exist. A logical law, the law of identity, states that everything is the same as itself: a tree is a tree, and a triangle is a triangle. This is often represented as A=A. Thinkers who hold this view, however, generally separate logic from other truths about things – for example, those of science or physics. One of the most crucial differences between logic and science is that scientific claims need to be confirmed by experiments. For example, if a scientific hypothesis expresses a certain fixed relationship between the temperature, the volume, and the pressure of all gases, then a series of experiments will confirm or deny this relationship. In addition, scientific laws, such as those embodied in Newtonian physics, can be superseded by others that are more comprehensive or powerful, such as Einstein's theory of relativity. It is not at all clear, however, how any experiment could confirm or falsify the most fundamental laws of logic, nor how new laws of logic could replace previous ones.

The second possibility claims that logic is true of our thinking as human beings. Logic is the way we, as humans, think. Logical laws may or may not be true of trees and other objects, but since logic is how we *must* think about things, it must hold true of our *thoughts* about trees. Logic would become the precondition for us to grasp and believe a theory about the world. Logic would appear to apply to all objects in the world because that is a requirement we place on things in order for them to be intelligible. Even if an object in the world were actually both circular and non-circular we could not *think* it. If part of the world were deeply illogical or contradictory we would never know it, because we cannot think contradictions. We would simply conclude that we hadn't yet formed the adequate theory to describe that part of the world and therefore should keep investigating.

Finally, there are those who hold that there could be a variety of logics.

These thinkers hold that some of us use a particular logic because of our culture or our language. Other people with significantly different cultures and languages use others. For us, the law of non-contradiction is as obvious as anything can be. For other peoples, this would not only appear problematic but might even appear false. This view seems to be a real possibility, yet it is not clear how we could get evidence that it is true. Consider a case in our own society. What if someone we met claimed that a specific object was both a tree and not a tree? Such a remark would undoubtedly surprise us and we would look for some explanation. However, we would not try to make sense of this statement by deciding that this person uses a different logic. Rather, we would begin to explore a number of other possibilities. Perhaps this person wasn't paying any attention to what he was saying, or perhaps he was making a joke. If neither of these options were available, we might consider other explanations. If nothing worked and the situation kept recurring, we might conclude that he or she does not know, has forgotten, or lost our language – specifically the meaning of the words "and" and "not". Either of these possibilities would be far more likely than the assertion that someone whose background is similar to our own was using a different logic in which contradictory claims were frequently made.

The question, then, is whether we would think differently about a group of people we might discover somewhere else in the world than we do about an individual in our own society. Suppose you are an anthropologist studying the language of a tribe. According to your translations of their sentences into English, they continually utter contradictions. However, they behave normally toward one another and seem to get along quite well in their everyday activities. How would we convince ourselves that they have a different logic and they do not appear as they do merely because we have mistranslated their language? This difficulty of coming to realize that another people might have a different, or at least a variant of our logic, is a constant problem hovering over anyone translating from one language to another. For nothing would be better evidence that we had failed at translating their language than to have most of their statements be of the sort we would consider logically absurd or strange.

Aristotle, who first investigated logic and made it systematic, held the first view: logic is true of all things. Boole, a 19th century logician, whose work we will consider in Unit XVI, held the second: logic is how we think. A question you might explore is how to make the third view reasonable.

The text for this unit is from *Metaphysics*. In it, Aristotle unambiguously states the law of non-contradiction and asserts that it is the most basic principle of everything that exists or can exist. Plato had previously proposed it in his work *The Republic*, but presented it only as an hypothesis. For Plato, the objects of mathematics – numbers and geometrical figures – were not contradictory, and anything similar to such objects was also covered by this principle. He was uneasy, however, about things which change and move. He was hesitant about claiming that trees, animals, stones, humans, and what we experience through our senses adhere to such a principle or law. Aristotle has no such hesitation. For him, it cannot be hypothetical that nothing can be both an *x* and not an *x*. In other words, for Aristotle, any observation or experience that seemed to disprove this principle would be itself automatically suspect. No experience or fact is more certain than this very principle. Therefore, if there were a conflict between an observation and this principle, we would surrender the supposed counter-example by doubting the accuracy of our observation.

Some people have expected a proof or demonstration of this principle. Such people, according to Aristotle, don't understand what they're asking for. Demonstrations and proofs must begin somewhere and he can think of no principle or claim that is a more appropriate place to begin. This is especially the case since demonstrations and proofs themselves depend on this principle. However, although he contends that non-contradiction can't be demonstrated, he does propose other characteristics of such a first principle. Such a principle or axiom must be the most familiar to us of all claims and cannot be based on anything else. Aristotle holds that this is true of the law of non-contradiction. It is the most familiar principle because we must first know this truth in order to know anything else. It can't depend on something else, because in order for anything else to be a specific thing, it must itself already be non-contradictory. However, some people – Aristotle mentions Heraclitus – don't merely ask for a proof or express doubt, but actually seem to deny this principle. Heraclitus had said, "Things taken together are whole and not whole, in tune and out of tune." Also, "Things in conflict are in agreement." These kinds of remarks appeared to deny the principle of non-contradiction. Faced with such an opponent, Aristotle responds that such a person cannot believe what he himself says. Heraclitus can *say* that he denies the principle of non-contradiction but he cannot *think* it, because that very thought is contradictory. This, of course, is circular, as Aristotle himself realizes. The question that emerges from this text is whether Aristotle or someone else can say enough to persuade us of the priority of this principle. Also, can people who disagree on this issue find a way to discuss it instead of simply launching into an endless debate on the subject or treating one another with an indifferent silence? In other words, how can we discuss a disagreement on the most fundamental principles of thinking and agreement?

TEXT

Aristotle: *Metaphysics*

Should either the mathematician or the scientist investigate the most fundamental principles and axioms of all things? Since these fundamental principles apply to all things and not only to numbers or geometrical figures, or to living and non-living things, mathematicians and scientists, as mathematicians and scientists, must assume them. They should not themselves investigate them. These principles must be investigated by a person who considers *all* things that exist and does not focus on a particular kind of thing. No one who studies or inquires into a specific subject matter should attempt to state whether these most fundamental principles of all things are true or false. In fact, mathematicians have never made this attempt, though some physicists have tried. They did so because they misunderstood their own subject. They thought their subject matter included everything that exists, and not just, as was in fact the case, only what happens in nature, or naturally. But since what exists naturally does not necessarily include all things, some one who thinks about how all things exist should be the one who undertakes to deal with these issues.

The most basic principle is the one that is most certain. Such a principle must be both the most familiar one and must also not be based on a hypothesis. We make errors about what is unfamiliar, and the most certain axiom must be one about which we cannot be wrong. Secondly, a hypothesis is based on another principle. But then, what it is based on would be more basic. But the fundamental principle of all things cannot rest on some other principle. It must, in some sense, be present or revealed in everything that exists. Since it must also be known by us in order for us to know anything else, it is the principle which is most familiar to us. Having now described who should investigate this principle and what it's like, we should state it.

The most basic principle is that it is impossible for the same attribute or quality at once to belong and not to belong to the same thing. This is the principle that possesses the characteristics we described above and is therefore the most certain. It is also impossible for anyone to deny it. No one can actually believe that the same thing is and is not. Some people imagine that Heraclitus did this because of some of the statements he made. What a person says, however, does not always represent what he believes. And we can show that this must be the case here. For contradictory attributes cannot belong to something at the same time in the same way. But opinions that contradict one another are contrary attributes. And believing something is holding an opinion. So it is impossible simultaneously to hold these

54

contrary opinions, though it is possible to claim that one does. It is possible to state a contradiction, but not possible to believe it.

Some people want a proof for this principle, but this is because they are confused about what they are demanding. It shows that they are ignorant both about proofs and demonstrations – about what we should try to prove and what we should not attempt to prove. For it is impossible that everything should have a proof. The process would go on endlessly to infinity, and then there would be no proof at all. So some things must be accepted without proof. If that is the case, what other principle do they think is a better candidate than the one we have proposed?

Even though we can't demonstrate this law, we can always refute an opponent who denies it if only that person will say something. If such a person makes no argument of his own, it is absurd for us to refute what we only imagine might be said. Such a person is really no better than a speechless plant. Such a proof by refutation differs from a simple proof. A simple proof would attempt to demonstrate this principle directly and would be circular. However, if someone else initiates the process by making some statement, a refutation can occur. A person who denies this principle must make a statement significant both to himself and others. Otherwise such a person can reason neither with himself nor with others. If he does this, however, he can be refuted, because he will already have accepted this very principle of non-contradiction. We can show that this principle is assumed in order to make a meaningful or significant statement. So though he appears to reject the principle, he already accepts it. And in addition, by making a statement he shows that he already accepts something without proof.

We can look at some consequences of denying this principle. If contradictory statements are true of the same thing at the same time, then all things will be one. For the same thing will be a ship, a wall, and a man, if it is possible both to affirm and to deny everything of an object. For if anyone thinks a man is not a ship, then he is not because he is not a ship. So everything is the same as everything else. From this example, we can see that without this principle, speech is impossible.

Questions

1. Which of the following examples are instances of a contradiction? Give a reason why or why not in each case.

    a) Two people put a hand into a bucket of water. One says it's cold; the other says it is warm.

    Contradictory   Non-Contradictory

    b) You put both hands into a bucket of water. Your left hand feels hot; your right feels cold.

    Contradictory   Non-Contradictory

    c) Two people are looking at two chairs. Both report accurately what they see but disagree on which chair is bigger.

    Contradictory   Non-Contradictory

    d) You see a single green chair in a room. When you return five minutes later there is a single red chair in the room.

    Contradictory   Non-Contradictory

    e) You see a green table. As you walk around it, the color changes. When you return to your original place the table is red.

    Contradictory   Non-Contradictory

    f) You and another person are standing in front of a table. You say it's green; the other person says it's red.

    Contradictory   Non-Contradictory

2. How could we convince ourselves that a group of people did not accept the law of non-contradiction?

3. What would the world be like if the law of non-contradiction were false?

4. Is the law of non-contradiction a truth about how things exist or a description of how we think?

VII

TALKING ABOUT THE INFINITE
TEXTS: Cantor, *Diagonal Proof*;
Wittgenstein, *Remarks on the Foundations of Mathematics*

Orientation:

One of the most crucial words in any language is the simple word "not". We cannot even imagine what it would be like without it. What would it mean to affirm, if we couldn't deny, or to choose, if refusal were not a possibility? And perhaps most importantly, how would we claim that two things were the same, if we couldn't claim they might be different? Denial, refusal, and difference all emerge from the word "not" or, in general, from negatives. When we assert that a horse is not a car, even if we know very little about horses and cars, we at least claim that they are different. Negation is so much a part of our language that sometimes we don't even notice it. Sometimes we even use the word "not" to try to state something positive. In words like "informal" and "invisible", we often feel we are naming something positive rather than claiming that an event or situation is not formal or not visible. There are even certain cases, e.g., impervious, which means not able to be penetrated or harmed, in which we don't use, or rarely use, the positive form. We rarely, if ever, say "pervious". Nowhere has the issue of how we use the word "not" been more problematic than in the subject matter that carries negation in its very name – the infinite. The question that arises is whether we can state anything positive about the infinite, or can we only state, in different ways, that it is not finite.

This issue comes to the forefront of mathematical concern through the work of Cantor, a recent account of whose approach we will consider in this lesson. Cantor feels that the infinite is a fertile and decisive field for mathematical exploration. Prior to Cantor, a merely negative way of speaking about the infinite seemed adequate. Attempts by previous mathematicians and philosophers to assert something definite and positive about the infinite led to paradox. All that seemed secure was to state that the infinite, whatever it was itself, was the not-finite. The infinite seemed to surround the finite as a kind of boundary, as the unknown world surrounded the known world

George Cantor (1845-1918) was born in St. Petersburg, Russia. He studied and taught in Germany. He created a new branch of mathematics with his work on set theory and the infinite. In 1884 he suffered a nervous breakdown, and thirty years later he died in an asylum.

Ludwig Wittgenstein (1889-1951) was born in Vienna, Austria, and studied engineering in Austria and England. In 1912, he began work on symbolic logic and created the propositional calculus. Most of his written work is devoted to investigating the relation between logic and language. His major works are *Tractatus Logico-Philosophicus, Philosophical Investigations,* and *Remarks on the Foundation of Mathematics.*

before Columbus. This approach, however, becomes inadequate once someone envisions the possibility of distinctly different infinites. The moment we try to speak about *different* infinites, we must state something positive about them in order to describe their difference, and not merely assert that neither is finite. It would be inadequate, for example, to state only that neither tables nor chairs are trees. To state merely that both are not trees does not assist someone in learning how to prepare for a dinner party. Yet precisely this – describing the difference between distinct infinites – was Cantor's problem.

Many groups of numbers appear infinite in the sense that they are not finite: the collection of natural numbers, 1,2,3,..., the collection of evens and odds, 2,4,6,...and 1,3,5,..., the collection of squares 1,4,9,16..., the collection of rationals, (numbers of the form m/n where m and n are both numbers like 1,2,3,4); and irrational numbers, $\sqrt{2}$, $\sqrt{3}$, and real numbers like 1.1414..., 1.14145..., 1.14146..., which are the collection of all the decimals which continue to infinitely many places. Are these groups all simply the infinite, the non-finite, or is each group different from the others? The merely negative way of speaking crumbles in the face of these questions, and one must make decisions about the positive use of words to continue. The first question which faces Cantor in his investigation into the nature of the infinite is, How large are these infinite groups or how many members do they contain?

It is not clear how to determine the number of members an infinite collection contains. We can't count them in any normal sense of counting, so if we wish to determine their quantity, some other method is necessary. We normally count objects by starting with the number 1 and then continuing through the sequence of cardinal numbers 1,2,3,... until we have gone through the entire group. The last number we reach tells us how many we have. However, there are other ways we can compare two groups. Suppose we have a collection of dollar bills and a collection of people. We distribute the bills to the people and when we finish each person has one dollar and there are no dollars left. We then know that there were as many dollars as people though we still don't know how many we had of either. We have established a one-to-one correspondence between the two groups. Though this doesn't give all the information we might want, it does give us some important data. If when we distributed the dollars, we had some left over, we would know that the number of dollar bills was larger than the number of people. This is the approach Cantor employs to compare infinite sets.

To accomplish this task requires that we choose a specific infinite set as our standard to compare with other groups. The counting numbers are selected. We will compare this group with some other group by attempting to establish a one-to-one correspondence between the two. To do this involves stating a rule which assigns each member of one group to a unique member of the first. For example, suppose we are comparing the counting numbers and the even numbers. The rule is: take each counting number and then double it. This shows that we can assign each member of the first group to a unique member of the second, and that there are none in the second group left out or left over. Since our standard group was the counting numbers, we say that the collection of even numbers is countable. By this we don't mean that we have actually counted them but that there are as many evens as counting numbers, since a one-to-one correspondence was established between the two groups. We can describe this fact by saying that the set of evens is "denumerable", which is a Latinized form of "countable". Let us next suppose that we can't establish such a correspondence, and that in fact we can show that some members of the second group must always be left over whenever we attempt a one-to-one correspondence. We then say the second group is *non-denumerable*, or "non-countable". Since some are left over, we are very tempted to state that the second group is "bigger". We can do the same thing for the squares, the cubes, and many other groups. It can also be done for the rational numbers, but in a more intricate way.

The first part of the text on Cantor shows how this is done for rational numbers. It employs the idea of a complete list. A list has a first item, a second item, a third item, and so on. The first item corresponds to the number 1 in our infinite group of counting numbers, the second corresponds to 2, the third to 3, and so on. Therefore, by showing a way of giving a unique place on the list to every member of the collection of rational numbers we supply the rule we need to create the one-to-one correspondence between the counting numbers and the rationals. Any infinite group of items that can be listed will be no different from the counting numbers, and will therefore itself be countable or denumerable.

The next part of the reading is intended as a proof that the real numbers, unlike the rationals, cannot be placed on such a list. This method of proof is what is called a reductio ad absurdum. With it we assume the opposite of what we are trying to prove, and show that this assumption leads to a contradiction. We are thus led to infer that its opposite is true. Let us suppose we have a complete list of the real numbers, that the group of reals is countable or denumerable. Cantor's proof presents a method of producing a real number different from every number on the list. Therefore, we always have a method of producing a real number that is not on the list. So we contradict our assumption that we have listed all the real numbers. The real numbers therefore cannot be listed. They are different from the other infinite groups we previously considered. Cantor then claims he has shown that the real numbers are not countable, that is, they are non-denumerable. Though this is also a negative expression and description, it appears somewhat more assertive than claiming that two groups are both not finite or infinite. It seems to assert *how* one group differs from the other, claiming that the real numbers form a larger collection than the other groups.

To see his proof more clearly we need to appreciate how a real number is written out. The real number system contains integers, rationals, and irrationals; for example, 2, $\frac{1}{2}$ $\sqrt{2}$. When these are written as real numbers, we write them as a decimal with infinitely many places after the decimal point. We write the integer 2 as 2.000... with infinitely many zeros. The rationals are of two sorts. For example, $5\frac{1}{4}$ or $\frac{21}{4}$ is 5.25000..., whereas $5\frac{1}{3}$ or $\frac{16}{3}$ is 5.333... In the first case, at some point the zeros are written to fill out the infinite places. In the second case, the same number or sequence of numbers repeats infinitely. An irrational, e.g., $\sqrt{2}$, written as a real number is 1.41421..., where the infinitely many numbers in the sequence never repeat.

Cantor's proof first assumes that the entire collection of real numbers has already been placed on a list and then gives a method for creating a real number which is not on the list. To create a number which is not on the list, he will systematically make it differ from every number on the list. To select the digit in the new number that will occupy the first place to the right of the decimal point, he considers the first number on the list. Suppose the digit in the first decimal place of the first number is a 3, e.g., 2.311... . He will choose a different digit for that decimal place in the new number, for example, 4. Then he considers the digit in the second decimal place of the second number on the list. Suppose that is a 5. He will select a digit different from that, for example, 7. This will become the second decimal place of the new number. Cantor's new number is now 0.47... . Each additional decimal place will be determined in a similar way. The new number differs, at least, in its first decimal place from the first number of the list, it differs in its second decimal place from the second number, and so on. The new real number differs from each real number on the list through this systematic set of changes; the number that is generated by this method is not on the list.

Cantor's proof shows something. But what does it show? Most mathematicians have accepted it and agreed that infinites can differ from one another and that the real numbers are "larger" than the counting numbers. Wittgenstein, whom many people consider one of the most seminal thinkers of the 20th century in logic, the foundations of mathematics, philosophy, and language, does not accept it as a proof. Some of his comments on Cantor's proof form the last part of this unit's reading, and can help focus the issues that emerge about Cantor's efforts. For example, do you think infinites can differ from one another in size, and can some be bigger than others? Wittgenstein feels that Cantor was tricked by language. Do you agree or do you think Cantor in fact produced a significant result? And is this result a positive assertion or a negative one? Are the reals bigger or more extensive than the counting numbers or are they simply different?

TEXTS

Cantor's Proof of Non-denumerability of the Real Numbers

Every positive rational number can be written in the form a/b, where a and b are integers, such as +2 or -3, and all these numbers can be put in an array with the rational number a/b in the ath column and the bth row. For example, $3/4$ is found in the third column and fourth row of the table below.

$$
\begin{array}{ccccc}
1/1 & 2/1 & 3/1 & 4/1 & 5/1 \\
1/2 & 2/2 & 3/2 & 4/2 & 5/2 \\
1/3 & 2/3 & 3/3 & 4/3 & 5/3 \\
1/4 & 2/4 & 3/4 & 4/4 & 5/4 \\
1/5 & 2/5 & 3/5 & 4/5 & 5/5
\end{array}
$$

All the positive rational numbers may now be arranged according to the following scheme: (In the array just defined we draw a zig-zag line that goes through all the numbers in the array. Starting at 1, we go horizontally to the next place on the right, obtaining 2 as the second member of the sequence, then diagonally down to the left until the first column is reached at the position occupied by ½, then vertically down one place to $1/3$, diagonally up until the first row is reached again at 3, across to 5, diagonally down to ¼, and so on, as shown in the figure. Travelling along this line we arrive at a sequence 1,2, $1/2, 1/3, 2/2$ 3, 4, $3/2, 2/3, 1/4, 1/5, 2/4, 3/3, 4/2,$ 5..., containing the rational numbers in the order in which they occur along the line. In this sequence we now cancel all those numbers a/b for which a and b have a common factor, so that each rational number *(r)* will appear exactly once and in its simplest form. Thus we obtain a sequence 1, 2, ½, $1/3$, 3, 4, $3/2, 2/3$, ¼, $1/5$, 5..., which can be numbered 1,2,3,4,5,6,7,8,9,10,11... . The sequence contains each positive rational number once and only once. This shows that the set of all positive rational numbers is denumerable since it corresponds to the set of counting numbers.

Since the rational numbers have been shown to be denumerable, one might suspect that *any* infinite set is denumerable, and that this is the ultimate result of the analysis of the infinite. This is far from being the case. Cantor made the very significant discovery that *the set of all real numbers* (rational and irrational), *is not denumerable.* In other words, the totality of real numbers presents a radically different and, so to speak, "higher" type of infinity than that of the integers or of the rational numbers alone. Cantor's ingenious indirect proof of this fact has become a model for many mathematical demonstrations. The outline of the proof is as follows. We start with the tentative assumption that all the real numbers have actually been denumerated in a sequence and listed. Then we exhibit a number that does not occur in the assumed denumeration. This provides a contradiction, since the assumption was that *all* the real numbers were included in the denumeration, and this assumption must be false if even one number has been left out. Thus the assumption that a denumeration of the real numbers is possible is shown to be untenable, and hence the opposite claim – Cantor's statement that the set of real numbers is not denumerable – is shown to be true.

To carry out this program, let us suppose that we have denumerated all the real numbers by arranging them in a table of infinite decimals, where the N's denote the integral parts and the small letters denote the digits after the decimal point.

$$
\begin{array}{llllllll}
\text{1st. number} & N_1 & a_1 & a_2 & a_3 & a_4 & a_5... \\
\text{2nd. number} & N_2 & b_1 & b_2 & b_3 & b_4 & b_5... \\
\text{3rd. number} & N_3 & c_1 & c_2 & c_3 & c_4 & c_5... \\
\text{4th. number} & N_4 & d_1 & d_2 & d_3 & d_4 & d_5...
\end{array}
$$

We assume that this sequence of decimal fractions contains *all* the real numbers. The essential point in the proof is now to construct by a "diagonal process" a new number, one that we can show to be not included in this sequence. To do this we first choose a digit a that differs from a_1, and is neither 0 nor 9 (to avoid possible ambiguities which may arise from equalities like 0.999... = 1000...), then a digit b different from b_2 and again unequal to 0 or 9, similarly c different from c_3, and so on. (For example, we might simply choose $a=1$ unless $a_1=1$, in which case we choose $a=2$, and similarly down the table for all the digits $b,c,d,e,...$). Now consider the infinite decimal:

$$z=N.abcde...$$

This new number z is certainly different from any one of the numbers in the table above; it cannot be equal to the first because it differs from it in the first digit after the decimal point; it cannot be equal to the second since it differs from it in the second digit; and, in general, it cannot be identical with the *n*th number in the table since it differs from it in the *n*th digit after the decimal point. This shows that our table of consecutively arranged decimals does *not* contain all the real numbers. Hence this set is not denumerable.

62

Wittgenstein: *Remarks on the Foundations of Mathematics*

1. Suppose someone says "Show me a number different from all of these," and as an answer he's given Cantor's diagonal rule. Why shouldn't he say, "But that's not what I meant. You haven't given me a number. You have merely given me a rule in words for the step-by-step construction of numbers that are different from each of these successively."?

2. The result of an arithmetical calculation that is expressed in words should be viewed suspiciously. A calculation makes clear the meaning of the expression in words. It is the finer or more precise instrument for showing what a mathematical expression in words really means, not the other way around.

3. Anyway, what can the concept "non-denumerable" be used for? A clever man got caught in this net of language.

4. The dangerous and deceptive theory about the claim, "The set of real numbers is non-denumerable," is that it makes what is the formation of an entirely new type of mathematical concept look like a fact of nature. We should always be suspicious when a proof like Cantor's proves more than its means seem to make possible. Something of this sort might be called a "puffed-up proof".

5. Suppose someone said, "When we think about Cantor's diagonal method of proof, we realize that we were misled by various analogies between different types of numbers. We thought that the concept of real numbers was similar to our concept of counting numbers, and that it made sense to try to compare them. But now we see we were wrong." To state this would be a mere straightforward and honest conclusion. But just the opposite happens. One pretends to compare the set of real numbers with the set of counting numbers. The difference in kind between two concepts is expressed by a strange form of expression as a difference in the size of the sets. We are then tempted to say the set of real numbers is bigger than the set of counting numbers.

6. Should we avoid the word "infinite" in mathematics? Yes, where it appears to give a meaning to a mathematical procedure instead of getting a meaning from it. And it would be silly to become disappointed if we find nothing infinite in arithmetic or mathematics. However, it is not silly to ask what gives the word "infinite" its meaning for us. Then we can go on to ask about its connection, if any, with these mathematical calculations in which it appears to play a part.

Questions

1.   Do you believe the following groups are finite or actually infinite?

	Finite	Actually infinite
numbers		
points on a line		
moments of time		
extent of time		
extent of space		
objects in the universe		

2.   Do you think that infinites can be larger or smaller than one another or do you feel they are all the same size? How would you order the collections you considered infinite in question #1 in regard to their size? What would be a way of defending your answer?

3.   Do you agree more with Cantor or Wittgenstein? Why?

VIII

HOW DO YOU SAY "I LOVE YOU" IN ARITHMETIC?

TEXT: Leibniz, *A Universal Language*

Orientation:

In the class discussions you have had while working with this book, you undoubtedly disagreed with some of the remarks and suggestions in the orientation sections. You probably also disagreed with some of what was stated in the texts, and with one another. The discussions frequently did not lead to conclusions, the arguments remained unsettled, and many of you found yourselves presenting varying points of view and perspectives rather than answers. This is rare, if not unique, in mathematics classes, where correct and incorrect answers are usually well-defined. Generally in mathematics classes, most of the speaking is done by the teacher, who knows the material. Some students become confused; others understand the concepts, strategies, and solutions. The latter generally speak to give correct answers, the former give incorrect answers when called on, or they ask for clarification. Your teacher's goal is that everyone completely understand the explanations and that everyone be capable of producing the correct answers. *Investigating Mathematics* does not change this goal, but extends it. Discussion, disagreement, and the presentation of different perspectives in mathematics, can reveal the context within which answers are correct and incorrect, and can enable all students to explore areas in mathematics in which it is not yet clear to *anyone* what the correct or incorrect answers are.

The goal of complete understanding has, in fact, been achieved for many members of our society in certain parts of mathematics – for example, addition in whole number arithmetic. Just about everyone can add whole numbers. Most of us also feel as confident in subtracting whole numbers from one another, especially when the result is a positive number. Though people have problems dealing with fractions, nonetheless those who do master them have a confidence and certainty that is rare in other fields. The same is true of other more complex fields of mathematics. Those who have mastered a particular field display a type of sureness in their use of it and in their agreement with one another that seems a model for us in other fields.

Gottfried Wilhelm Leibniz (1647-1716) was born in Leipzig, Germany. Leibniz wrote on mathematics, physics, theology, philosophy, law, and history. A co-inventor of the calculus, he also was one of the first to investigate symbolic logic. In physics he was a great advocate of the importance of conservation laws. His most important works are *The Discourse on Metaphysics*, *The Essay on Nature*, and *The Monadology*.

Wouldn't you desire the same degree of certainty and mutual understanding among people as that which we find when we compare our results of adding a few integers?

It is therefore not surprising that people in other fields of study, and all of us, when we are not understood by others in our daily lives, often look upon mathematics with a kind of envy and try to imitate procedures. Some have looked to careful definitions of key terms as the answer. Some try to state clearly and explicitly the fundamental assumptions they employ. Others go further in articulating their theories by imitating the kind of proofs found in mathematics. This effort has had some success. Physicists and chemists can often agree with one another about their subjects. As one looks at biology, psychology, history, and language studies, however, the level of agreement among equally trained professionals diminishes. And even in the cases where scientific understanding and agreement is greatest, this effort has had little effect on daily life. When they are not doing physics and mathematics, physicists and mathematicians misunderstand, disagree, and argue with one another as often as the rest of us. Scientists and mathematicians, in spite of a high degree of professional agreement, still have personal conflicts, and when they are from different countries, almost always take their own country's side in war. This level of disagreement and conflict is what Leibniz attempts to deal with in this week's text.

Leibniz was one of the most creative mathematicians and scientists. He and Newton independently created the calculus, a form of mathematics initially devised to capture the movements and changes of objects. The calculus soon became the foundation of mathematical physics. But though Leibniz was deeply involved in the very field characterized by agreement, and was a crucial contributor in spreading that kind of agreement into science, his own life was pervaded by conflict and controversy, particularly by disagreements with Newton. These two men struggled and fought with one another about who first created the calculus and about what was the proper form and symbolism to employ in its presentation. Newton is now generally awarded the honor of its creation, though Leibniz's general approach and symbolism is what you will use when you study that part of mathematics. It is therefore somewhat ironic that the most radical suggestion for utilizing the model of mathematics to further human community, agreement, and the growth of knowledge came from someone who rarely experienced it himself and who died in solitude with hardly anyone to mourn his passing.

Leibniz's dream was to try to base all of our thinking on an arithmetical model. However, he did not merely wish to *imitate* mathematics in other fields of study or in our daily concerns, issues, and activities, but to turn all of our words and thoughts into numbers. He wanted to go beyond giving definitions of key terms, getting agreement on fundamental principles or axioms, and utilizing logical proofs. He conceived of the complete transformation of our thinking through the construction of a perfect language based on arithmetic. He hoped to create a language in which all our concepts would be named by numbers, a language in which the relations between these ideas would be represented and revealed by arithmetical relations. We would then think about everything with the same confidence and agreement we now have when we figure out how many apples can be purchased for two dollars if each apple costs 25 cents. Many thinkers have attributed human conflicts to the fact of multiple languages, and have felt that if we all spoke the same language, disagreement would cease. This belief, however, brings into question what it would mean to possess the "same" language. Since we know of civil wars in England and America, the fact that all people might speak one language, e.g., English, hardly encourages much optimism. English speakers, even though they speak the "same" language might use words differently and hold different beliefs. They would ultimately be similar to people using different languages. Having the same language involves a deeper identity than the similarity between two English speakers. Both the words and the most fundamental beliefs of the people must be identical. To insure that identity, however, the concepts in our minds, how they relate to objects in the world, and the words that represent them must all be shared by everyone. It is at this stage of the problem that mathematics and particularly arithmetic holds the solution for Leibniz.

Numbers, for Leibniz, are perfect names. The number 3, for example, is the perfect name for our concept of three and for all the groups of three things in the world. Similarly for all numbers. To appreciate why he might think this, we merely need to notice what happens in arithmetic. We *all* agree that 3x2=6 and that 12x12=144. In addition, when we know we have 12 groups of 12 objects, we are immediately in complete agreement with both reality and with other people. We *all* conclude that we have 144 objects and that we would laboriously discover this fact if we counted them. This is what Leibniz desired for all names and words. If we could only find the proper numbers for the concepts of things, we would possess a language that would guarantee agreement among people and the continual development of our knowledge. The questions that emerge are: Is such a language possible? If it is possible, is it desirable?

In the two selections, Leibniz sets out his view of the problem, his outlines for its solution, and some of his ideas about how such a language would be constructed. The principle issues are how to represent by numbers the words of terms that correspond to our concepts, and then how to combine the numbers for these terms into more complex structures and into statements. His underlying claim is that the various complex grammatical structures that we find in language and that we utilize in speaking and writing can all be transformed into a linguistic form that can be translated into arithmetical and algebraic equations. The essential aspect of an equation is the equal sign, =. This, Leibniz construes as the verb "to be". The first step in Leibniz's attempt is therefore the assumption that any true or false sentence can be rewritten as a relation between a subject and a predicate linked by "is" or "are". This verb is then equivalent to the equal sign. The next task is to assign characteristic numbers to the words or terms in the subject and predicate of the transformed sentence in order that each sentence take the form of an equation.

In order to find characteristic numbers for terms, certain other assumptions must be made. Numbers have a variety of characteristics and relations with one another – some numbers are odd, some are even, some perfect squares, others cubes, some numbers are prime, and other numbers can be factored into their prime components. These last two characteristics are what Leibniz wishes to utilize as the basis for his language. Since all numbers are either prime, such as 1,2,3,5,7,11,13, etc., or composite, such as 8, 26, and 32, we must establish a comparable division among words or terms and the concepts they stand for. Prime numbers would correspond to certain terms or words, other words would correspond to the composite numbers built up from these primes by multiplication. The key to the distinction between the terms is definition. Some terms, the most general terms that apply to all things – such as "being", "thing", and "unity" – are indefinable because they are so general. They are therefore assigned prime numbers. Other terms are defined by means of these concepts. Their characteristic numbers are established by multiplying the prime numbers that correspond to the terms in their definition. Leibniz's example uses the definition, "man is a rational animal." If we assign the number 2 to "rational" and 3 to "animal", the characteristic number of man is 6. "Man is a rational animal" is then the equation "6=2x3". Of course, this example assumes that we have not yet defined "rational" and "animal". When we establish definitions for those terms, they will be given new characteristic numbers. The number for man will therefore be different but will still remain the product of numbers in its definition. The statement, "man is a rational animal" in Leibniz's new language becomes the equation, (number for man) = (number for rational) x (number for animal).

If we suppose that this brief exposition and Leibniz's treatment shows us that such an approach is possible, we must ask whether we desire it. What would we be like as people if we used such a language? For example, could we have poetry in such a language? Poetry involves metaphors, but could such Leibnizean names or numbers be used metaphorically? If they could, wouldn't we be back in the very situation from which we began in relation to conflict and disagreement? So we must ask whether mathematics is really a model for all human activities, and if not, which ones should be approached in this way. What would be lost to us if Leibniz's dream came true? What would you want a perfect language to accomplish, and which of the difficulties we face with our own language would you want it to overcome?

TEXTS

Leibniz: *The Method of the Mathematicians*

Happiness consists in peace of mind. Lasting peace of mind depends on our confidence in the future. Such confidence is based on science. Science is therefore necessary for true happiness. Science, however, depends on demonstrations, but the discovery of such proofs by a reliable method is not known to everyone. Each person is able to judge demonstrations, but not everyone can discover them or present them clearly to others. The true method for creating demonstrations, in its full scope and power, is entirely unknown. It has only been practiced to a limited extent, and then only in mathematics.

Though the mathematical method has not enabled mathematicians to discover all mathematical truths, it has saved them from mistakes. They have, at least, not said anything false. If other thinkers had imitated mathematicians on this point, we should all be quite content. Our knowledge would be vastly increased in physics, medicine, and in everything required for a happy and contented life. The reason why this science of demonstrations has until now been found only in mathematics is not generally understood. If the cause of the problem were known, the remedy would have been discovered. The reason is this: Mathematics carries its own test with it. If someone states a false claim in mathematics, I can check it immediately. All I have to do is calculate with pen and paper to discover the error, however small it may be. If it were only this simple in other matters, we would not have so many conflicting opinions. But experiments in science are difficult and costly, and they are impossible in the most important issues of our lives.

This difficulty is not insurmountable. If you take the trouble to consider what I am about to say, you may, in fact, agree. The tests made in mathematics to guard against mistakes are not made on the things themselves. They are made on the symbols we have substituted for the thing. Take, for example, a numerical calculation. If 1677 times 365 are 612,105, we would never have reached this result if we had to make 365 piles of 1677 pebbles each and then count all of them. Instead we use the symbols and paper and pen. So it is obvious that if we could find symbols to express all our thoughts as definitely as arithmetical symbols express numbers or geometrical analysis represents lines, we could, in all subjects, which can be reasoned about, accomplish as much as is achieved in arithmetic and geometry. All inquiries that depend on our reasoning would then be performed by a manipulation and calculation with symbols. This would enable us immediately to discover many important truths. We would be sure of accomplishing everything a given set of facts allows.

These symbols, which accurately express all our thoughts, would constitute a new language. It could be written and spoken. This language would be difficult to construct, but easy to learn. It would be so useful that everyone would accept it and would make communications among all people possible and simple. Those who use this language would never make mistakes as long as they can avoid errors of calculation. In addition, the language would silence ignorant people. People would only speak or write about what they understand. If they did otherwise, one of two things would happen. The arrogance and ignorance of their statements and claims would be obvious to everyone. Or they would learn something by speaking or writing. This happens now in arithmetic, where those who calculate sometimes meet with a success they didn't imagine. This would especially happen with our language because of its exactness. This language would be the greatest tool of the human mind. This project is the most important task for all people and for the greatest thinkers. When this is accomplished, it will simply be up to us to be happy. We will have an instrument that will perfect our reason at least as much as the telescope has perfected our vision.

Leibniz: *Elements and Rules of Characteristic Numbers*

A term is the subject or predicate of a statement that is formed with the verb "to be". To every such term we must assign a characteristic number. There is one rule for discovering suitable characteristic numbers. Suppose the concept of a term or word is directly built up out of the concepts of two or more other terms. The number of the given term is produced by multiplying the characteristic numbers of the terms composing it. For example, consider the truth, "man is a rational animal." If the number of "animal" is 2 and the number of "rational" is 3, the number of "man" will be 2x3, or 6.

We shall introduce letters such as "a" for animal, "r" for rational and "m" for man when numbers are not given or at least need not be considered specifically. This is just like in algebra, where it is a way of avoiding the effort to show for each individual case what can be shown at once for an infinite number of instances. The sentence, "man is a rational animal," then becomes, "m=axr".

This single rule is enough to include everything in our new language if we have a distinct and clear concept of it. That is, if we know its component parts and can distinguish it from everything else after considering its parts. In other words, we can produce a characteristic number if we can give a definition for the term. For the concepts we have of the terms that make up the definition are what build up the concept we have of the thing. Moreover, we can distinguish most things from one another because their component parts differ. We rarely must concern ourselves with how the parts are ordered in relation to one another in order to distinguish two things. Completely general terms that are indefinable are assigned prime numbers.

In those cases when we can't decide or have not yet discovered the parts of a thing, we temporarily assign the thing a previously unused prime number as its characteristic number. The fact that a prime number has no factors or parts represents to us that we don't yet have clear and distinct concepts of its components. This still allows us, however, to represent all the true statements into which this term enters and to demonstrate them logically. Assigning a prime number when we don't know the parts is similar to what Euclid does with this definition of a straight line. Though Euclid defines straight line as a line that lies evenly with the points on itself, he nowhere uses this definition in his proofs. Instead he uses more definite claims, his postulates, about straight lines. Archimedes tried to go farther and analyze the straight line. He defined it as the least distance between two points. In this way he could give more adequate proofs for what Euclid had already demonstrated without an adequate definition. In the same way we can demonstrate truths even when we cannot yet give a complete definition of terms, and then prove them again later when the appropriate characteristic number is discovered.

To clarify the relations of characteristic numbers in statements, we must keep the following in mind. Every true statement involves a relation between a subject and a predicate. The subject and predicate are related as part to whole, whole to part, or whole to whole, when they are the same or identical. In the sentence, "gold is a metal," "gold" is the subject, "metal", the predicate. Understood logically, gold is contained as a part in the larger class of metals. In our new language, however, metal is contained as a part in gold because the characteristic number of "gold" is the subject, "metal", the predicate. Understood logically, gold is contained as a part in the larger class of metals. In our new language, however, metal is contained as a part in gold because the characteristic number of "gold" contains as a factor the number assigned to "metals". The smaller or more definite logical class has the larger characteristic number because more terms with their characteristic numbers are needed to define it. The most general and universal terms would then have the smallest numbers.

Two terms that contain each other and yet are equal in extent are coincident terms whose relation is whole to whole. For example, the concept of triangle coincides with the concept of trilateral. Whatever is contained in one is contained in the other, though they have different definitions. Nonetheless, their characteristic numbers will be the same. We can also determine through characteristic numbers when one term is contained in another. We need only test whether one number exactly divides the other. For example, if the characteristic number of man is found to be 6 and that of ape is 10, it is obvious that neither concept is contained in the other since they don't divide one another exactly. We can recognize, however, that both are animals, since 6 and 10 are both divided by 2, which we previously considered the characteristic number of the concept "animal".

Questions

1. Many thinkers have modeled their work on the procedure of mathematics. They imitate mathematics either because they begin by using definitions, by stating fundamental assumptions clearly, or by employing proofs in their presentation. In the fields listed below, which of these characteristics would you desire? You may check more than one.

	Defs.	Clearly Stated assumptions or axioms	Proofs	None of these
Law				
Physics				
Literature				
Politics				
Religion				

2. Describe briefly a problem between people caused by language. What change or changes in our language would protect us? A recent example of such an issue is the use of "he" to refer to both men and women.

3. Do you think human conflict would cease if we had a perfect language? What do you think a perfect language would be like?

73

LOGICAL EQUIVALENCE IN MATHEMATICS

IX

TEXTS: *Euclid's Parallel Postulate and Seven Alternatives*

Orientation:

Like other human beings, mathematicians often disagree. Unlike the normal disagreements that we encounter daily about questions of fact or superficial opinions, however, mathematical disagreements are more like disagreements in politics. It is rare that mathematicians disagree about whether a particular theorem is true. This is possible, though in those cases the disagreement is generally about whether a certain type of proof is legitimate: some mathematicians refuse to utilize certain methods of argument that others are willing to accept. An example is what is called a *"reductio ad absurdum"* proof. A *reductio ad absurdum* proof – a reduction to absurdity – is an approach we often use with one another in ordinary disagreements. If you and I disagree about something, I might try to convince you by proving to you that I am right. Sometimes, however, I will try to convince you that what you believe is absurd. My idea is that by showing you that your belief must be wrong you will be persuaded that my position must be right. Some mathematicians accept this indirect type of proof, but others hold that only direct proofs are allowable. This sort of conflict is really a disagreement about a method of proof, even though it takes the form of a disagreement about a particular theorem.

Mathematicians' conflicts, however, are generally different from this sort of issue about logic. They are like the conflicts we call ideological when they are in the political realm. These are of two types. One type concerns the nature of mathematics. Sometimes one mathematician will claim that the work of another is not really mathematics – that it is not sufficiently rigorous to be legitimately called mathematics. In the 18th century this occurred about the calculus. It was prompted by the paradoxes which emerge about the infinitesimal. These oppositions are similar to the ones we encounter between Marxism and Capitalism. The conflicts are so basic (in the political case it is about human nature, in the other it is about mathematics itself)

Euclid (C. 350-275 B.C.) was a Greek mathematician who taught at Alexandria in Egypt, a great center of learning in the ancient world. Best known for his great work on geometry - *Elements* - he also wrote on conic sections, astronomy, optics, and music. Many philosophers and mathematicians have held that Euclid's *Elements* is one of the most influential works ever written, both for its content and as a model of thinking.

that such arguments generally lead nowhere. The rivals stop talking to one another. Instead, they try to convince others who are neutral to become their adherents.

The second type of disagreement, which is more typical and also about fundamental issues, is more similar to the differences in our own country between Democrats and Republicans. These political parties certainly agree on fundamental matters concerning democratic processes and the importance of the Constitution, but they hold opposing views on almost every issue we face in our daily lives. The text for today will concern this second type of disagreement.

All of the mathematicians whose differences of opinion we will consider today agree on one major issue. They all agree that Euclid's geometry is true. They accept all the truths of Euclidian geometry; both the postulates he presents and the theorems he proves from them. In other words, we are not in the situation where a mathematician claims that certain Euclidian theorems or postulates are false, or that Euclidian geometry is not really mathematics. For example, none of these mathematicians are claiming that parallel lines get closer and closer to one another, or that more than one straight line can be drawn between two points. To make these claims would be to advocate a non-Euclidean geometry, a geometry that is entirely different from the Euclidian one. All of the mathematicians we will consider in this unit present Euclidian geometry, but they disagree with the way in which Euclid himself presented it. They don't disagree about which mathematics is true, but about how to do it and how to present it. They disagree on the way in which the truths are interconnected, not on the truths themselves. This type of disagreement would be very strange in certain fields of activity. We may like or dislike a poem or a symphony, but we would probably not say we or someone else should rewrite it or recompose it, though we might very well claim that one reading or performance of it is preferable. In other fields, such claims are more common. They often occur in science or in history or in courts of law. In these cases, everyone could agree on all the facts, but disagree on how they are interconnected. It is revealing about our beliefs to try the following imaginative exercise. Read the short poem on the next page.

Poem - by William Carlos Williams

As the cat
climbed over
the top of

the jamcloset
first the right
forefoot

carefully
then the hind
stepped down

into the pit of
the empty
flowerpot

Now try to rewrite it so that you feel it still says or accomplishes what the poet meant or intended. You will probably feel you failed. The various reasons for your failure will show you some of the beliefs we hold about mathematics, where such paraphrases are not only possible but common.

Euclid's fifth postulate has given rise to many profound investigations into mathematics. Euclid develops his geometry from five postulates. He offers no proof of these postulates, nor does he present the reader with any explanation. He simply postulates five geometrical claims as his beginning. The first four – 1) that we can draw a line, 2) extend it to any length, 3) draw a circle of any radius, and 4) that all right angles are equal – are relatively straightforward. There are interesting issues to raise about each of these, but these questions are eclipsed by the puzzles that emerge about the fifth. The fifth postulate states: *if two lines cross a third, and the interior angles are less than two right angles, then the first two lines will meet on that side.* The complexity of the language of the fifth postulate sharply distinguishes it from the others. But further, it is not even clear what the real content of the postulate is. Is it a postulate about when three lines form a triangle, or is it instead a postulate about when they don't form such a figure? In other words, is it about triangles or about parallel lines?

Most mathematicians viewed the fifth postulate as a attempt to state a postulate about parallel lines rather than one about triangles. They therefore wondered why it was stated so indirectly. Some mathematicians thought Euclid's motive might have been to articulate a truth about lines that actually meet, and about which we might have some intuition, rather than about parallels, lines that *never* meet. This would be like using our knowledge of the finite, about which we feel we know something, in order to prove truths about the infinite. Other mathematicians felt this postulate sounded more like a theorem that should be proved than a postulate or axiom that we must accept in order to proceed. They therefore tried to turn it into a theorem by proving it from the other four postulates, or from the other four plus a new simpler fifth postulate. Many mathematicians, however, decided simply to replace it with a postulate explicitly about parallel lines that was logically equivalent to the fifth postulate. Two statements or postulates are logically equivalent when using either of them we can prove the other one, or using either of them along with the other four postulates, we can prove the other statement.

This unit's text presents seven such postulates that different mathematicians have used as alternatives to the original fifth postulate. Each of these is logically equivalent to the fifth postulate, and therefore also logically equivalent to the others. Any of these postulates along with the original four leads to the others as a theorem. These theorems can also be utilized in proofs to prove yet other theorems, the remaining theorems derived from these logically equivalent but different sets of postulates will be the same. The choice of one set of five postulates instead of another logically equivalent set is therefore not based on an attempt to enlarge the group of proved theorems, but on some other consideration. Such considerations could be of various kinds. For example:

a) a certain version could be more obviously true,
b) it could reveal a more central aspect of parallel lines or the space in which the geometry holds,
c) it could be more useful as a teaching device,
d) it could possess a grammatical or conceptual simplicity, or
e) it could fit better with the other postulates.

You might also imagine other possibilities.

To see briefly that these alternatives are logically equivalent, we can sketch out a sample set of proofs. We will first assume one of the postulates, and then prove one of the others. Then, we will reverse the sequence. We will take alternatives #3 and #4 for our example. Alternative #3 states: two straight lines that intersect one another cannot both be parallel to the same straight line. #4 states: two straight lines parallel to the same straight line are parallel to each other.

Let's assume #3. Lines AB and CB intersect at point B. Assume BC is parallel to DE.

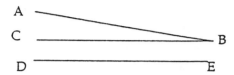

By this postulate, AB cannot also be parallel to DE. If it were parallel to DE, it therefore could not intersect BC. It would therefore also be parallel to BC. But that is the same as alternative #4, which states that two lines parallel to the same straight line are parallel to one another.

Now let's start with #4. If straight lines AB and CD are parallel to line EF, then they are parallel to each other.

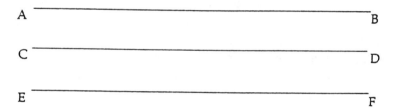

Assume they are both parallel to EF but intersect. But that violates alternative #3 which states that two intersecting lines cannot both be parallel to the same straight line. So if we assume alternative #4, then alternative #3 must follow from it. In a similar way, each of these alternatives is equivalent to the others. Since they are all logically equivalent, if one is false, all of them are false. So your preference for one cannot be based on whether it is true but on other considerations, such as obviousness, simplicity, utility, or some other characteristic.

The alternatives fall into two groups: 1-5 concern parallel lines, but 6 and 7 deal with facts about triangles. To appreciate the connection between the two groups, we can consider alternative #7. "Given any figure, there exists a figure similar to it of any size we please." Let us consider the specific case of a triangle.

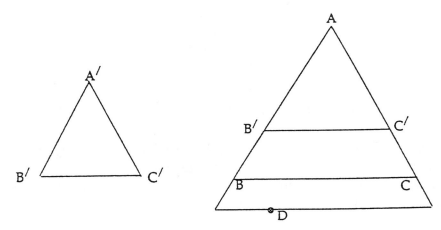

When we have two similar triangles, A' B' C' and ABC, one is larger than the other. If a vertex A' of the smaller triangle is placed on the corresponding vertex A of the larger, the bases of B' C' and BC of the triangles will be parallel. If there were a maximum size for similar triangles, say ABC, then through those points beyond the maximum figure, say D, no line could be drawn parallel to the base B' C' of the other triangle because it would result in a larger similar triangle when we extend lines AB and AC. However, this contradicts alternative #2 which states that through any point a line parallel to another straight line can be drawn.

These seven alternatives were presented by mathematicians because they all agreed that Euclid's fifth postulate was defective. They disagree, however, about the logically equivalent alternative which should replace it. Each suggestion represents a mathematician's decision about the most appropriate approach to Euclidian geometry. In comparing the entire group, a useful method of deciding which you would prefer is to ask yourself which would surprise you the most if it were shown to be false.

TEXT

Euclid's Fifth Parallel Postulate and Seven Alternatives

Euclid: If a straight line falls on two other straight lines making the sum of the interior angles on the same side of the first straight line equal to less than two right angles, then those two lines, if produced indefinitely, will meet on that side on which the interior angles are less than two right angles.

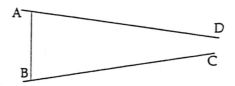

If angle ABC + angle DAB < 2 rt. angles,
then AD and BC produced will meet toward D and C.

* * * * * * * *

Alternative #1: If a line AB crosses two others, AD and BC, and the angles made equal 2 right angles, the two lines AD and BC will be parallel.

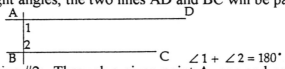

Alternative #2: Through a given point A, one and only one parallel line CB can be drawn to another given straight line DE.

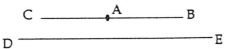

Alternative #3: Two straight lines AB and BC which intersect one another cannot both be parallel to one and the same straight line DE.

80

Alternative #4: Straight lines AB and CD parallel to the same straight line EF are parallel to one another.

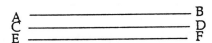

Alternative #5: There exist straight lines AB and CD that are everywhere equidistant from one another.

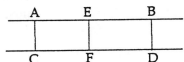

AC = BD=EF

Alternative #6: There exists a triangle in which the sum of the three angles is equal to two right angles.

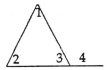

angle 1 + angle 2 + angle 3 = angle 3 +angle 4=180°

Alternative #7: Given any figure, there exists a figure similar to it of any size we please.

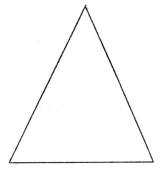

Questions

1. Below is a list of reasons for choosing or not choosing one alternative to the fifth postulate over the others. For each alternative check how it compares with the fifth postulate.

Alternative postulates listed by number	Obviously true		Useful for Teaching		Informative about geometry	
	More	Less	More	Less	More	Less
1.						
2.						
3.						
4.						
5.						
6.						
7.						

2. Imagine yourself a mathematician setting out postulates for a school textbook of Euclidian geometry. Would you keep Euclid's fifth postulate, or would you choose an alternative? Give a reason for your decision.

3. If all these alternatives and the fifth postulate were false, which would you find most surprising? Why?

X

HOW ARE MATHEMATICAL TRUTHS TRUE?
TEXT: Kant, *Prolegomena to Any Future Metaphysics*

Orientation:

      Mathematics has often been held up as a model of human knowledge. Unlike when we talk about a poem, a movie, or a sports team, it seems possible with mathematics to come to agreement about what theorems are true. We frequently disagree about the meaning of a poem, whether one movie is better than another, or who is the best player on a team. But when we disagree about a particular mathematical issue – about how to factor an equation or about whether a certain property holds of a triangle – we can invariably resolve the disagreement though we may continue to disagree about how the truths we accept should be organized. This special characteristic of mathematics has always struck people as remarkable and worth thinking about. Even science and history are subject to honest and genuine disagreements that we cannot easily resolve. Scientists differ about the significance of experimental results and about the relation between a series of experiments and a theory. Historians can agree about events and facts, but differ dramatically about the cause of an event – for example, the cause of a war. Even eyewitnesses to the "same event" often differ in their accounts of it. The fact that there can be this sort of universal agreement in mathematics is one reason that many people have considered mathematics a model of human knowledge. Universal agreement about the truth of a statement has sometimes been considered the difference between knowledge and mere opinion.

      Another aspect of mathematical truth that many people have noted is its relation to our daily experience. Though it may be that the perception or experience of certain shapes or the addition of objects – e.g., adding 2 apples to 3 apples and getting 5 apples – may have given rise to certain mathematical concepts or theorems, once these theorems or concepts emerge they seem independent of future experience, unlike in the sciences. In other words, if we measured the angle sum of a number of triangular objects with a protractor, and we found that sometimes they equaled 179° and sometimes 181°. We don't conclude that triangles have variable angle sums which hover around 179°- 181°. Instead, we would probably say that the objects we measured were not perfect triangles, but only approximately triangular. In other

---

Immanuel Kant (1724-1804) was born in Königsberg, Germany. He studied at the university there and became its Professor of Logic and Metaphysics in 1770. In his major work – the *Critique of Pure Reason* (1781) – he attempts to describe the conditions under which it is possible for us to know anything. This work focused all philosophical thinking since then on this issue. In addition, he wrote on cosmology, morality, beauty, and scientific theories.

words, we would claim that the sides or edges of the figures were not really straight lines. In short, experience may agree with mathematical theorems, but when it doesn't agree, we neither throw out the theorem nor disregard the experience. We view the theorem and the experience as independent of one another.

A third aspect of mathematics is that many of its results are neither obvious nor self-evident. Though some of its theorems or axioms seem hardly worth thinking about or proving, many of them are surprising. Could anyone have anticipated the Pythagorean theorem or the quadratic equation? Mathematics, like history and science, teaches us new facts. In this regard it is unlike logic, which often seems to spell out in detail what we already implicitly know.

As a model of what it is to know or what a truth is, mathematics thus brings up three characteristics: 1) people agree on it, 2) once you know it, future experience cannot convince you it is false, and 3) it is informative. Kant accepts these three characteristics, though you might disagree with some or all of them. In fact, he comes close to accepting them as the model of what real knowledge should look like, though he doesn't go quite that far. The task he sets himself in this text is to explain, or to give an account of, these characteristics and, to a certain extent, to defend them.

Kant approaches this issue as a mathematician might approach his own subject. He uses a technical vocabulary, defining it carefully in order to give his arguments a kind of mathematical rigor. Kant argues that mathematics occupies a kind of middle place between truths we establish purely by thinking, as in logic, and facts about experience, as in science and history. An example of the first kind of truth might be the entirely uninteresting statement that a tree is a tree, or that a statement cannot be both true and false at the same time and in the same respect. An example of an experiential truth might be that Lincoln was assassinated, or that the earth is about 25,000 miles in circumference. As we will see, Kant believes he has no difficulty explaining these two kinds of truth. Mathematical truth, however, seems to have some characteristics of each: it combines the certainty of logical truths with the interesting newness of scientific and historical facts. This intermediate type of truth Kant calls "synthetic *a priori*". In order to give an account of mathematics, then, Kant must explain a type of truth that is a hybrid of the other two types. However, explaining how such a hybrid is possible is a difficult problem because truths of logic and truths of experience seem to have characteristics that are mutually exclusive and even opposed to each other.

To see what this means, we can give a brief account of his approach. Kant focuses on the judgments we make. (A judgment is merely any sentence that can be true or false.) To Kant, all judgments consist of a subject and a predicate. In the judgment, "A body is extended," "body" is the subject and "extended" is the predicate. In the judgment, "A straight line is the shortest distance between two points," "A straight line" is the subject; and "the shortest distance between two points", is the predicate. For Kant, the question of how to describe a truth becomes the question: What is the relation between the subject and the predicate?

According to Kant, this relation can be of two kinds: analytic or synthetic. In an analytic judgment, we analyze the subject and discover that the predicate is already there. For example, consider the statement, "An uncle is a man." When we analyze "uncle" we necessarily find "man" since every person who is an uncle must be a man. The judgement is therefore analytic. In a synthetic judgment we don't find the predicate in the subject, so we must synthesize them, or put them together. For example, if we consider the sentence, "The earth is 25,000 miles in circumference," no amount of analyzing the concept "earth" will yield "25,000 miles in circumference". To find that out we need some way of measuring it. It is therefore synthetic or put together by us through what we learn from experience.

Of course, we must ask how we analyze and how we synthesize. Kant gives his own example of what he means. An instance for him of an analytic truth is, "Bodies are extended in space." Though when we think about bodies, this fact may not be the one most present to our minds, it becomes clear when we think more attentively about the concept "body". If we think carefully about bodies, we will realize that being in space or being extended is part of the concept. We can test this by examining whether the statement, "A body is not extended" violates the logical law of non-contradiction. That is, we must ask whether we can give meaning to the sentence, "A body is not extended." It seems that we simply cannot even think the sentence. For Kant, this means that the concept or thought of a body already contains the concept "extended". Because it does, no further experience is necessary.

Kant's example of a synthetic judgment is, "Bodies have weight." Since weight depends where a body is on earth or in the universe – some could be weightless – no logical analysis could extract the predicate "weight" from the concept "body". In order to do it, we must check out the body experientially. We must put it on a scale of some kind. In other words, in this case, an experience enables us to put together the subject and predicate. Since analytic truths are prior to experience, he calls them *"a priori"*, the Latin for "prior to". Thus, "All bodies are extended in space," Kant calls analytic *a priori*. "All bodies have weight," he calls synthetic *a posteriori*, because the judgement can only be made after (*a posteriori)* some experience.

Kant claims that mathematical truths are like the truths of logic in that they are prior to any particular experience, or *a priori*. However, they are also like the truths of experience in that we must look to some object other than our mere ideas or concepts to determine their truth. In other words these truths are synthetic as well. Before him, he claims, no thinker had recognized this. The examples Kant uses to

85

defend this claim about mathematics are "7+5 = 12," and, "The straight line is the shortest distance between two points." He claims that, in each case, the relation between the subject and the predicate is synthetic. In the first case, he claims you can analyze the subject "7 + 5" as much as you want and never discover the predicate "12". In the second, his claim is that the concept "straight line" does not contain the predicate "shortest". For both of these examples, you need to look somewhere else to put the subject and predicate together. Kant accounts for the fact that mathematical truth is interesting, surprising, or informative by the claim that it is synthetic. Yet like logic, it is prior to all experience. It does not depend on experience as was necessary to determine a body's weight. We need only internally visualize, or imagine, mathematical axioms and postulates to recognize their truth. In addition, it is possible for us all to agree because mathematics is primarily a fact about all human beings. Mathematics is a fact about how we must think about, imagine, and experience the world. It is therefore *a priori*.

This brings up several questions. Do we agree that mathematics is neither like logic nor science, or would we prefer to view it as one of these, or more like one of these? If it is like neither, is Kant's explanation helpful? In other words, should we explain mathematical truth through a special relation between the subject and predicate? What is there that might be like experience in allowing the synthesis, but like logic in being prior to experience? Kant's suggestion is that it is our imaginations. What do you think of this possibility? Which is the better example for this point – arithmetic or geometry?

TEXT

Kant: *Prolegomena To Any Future Metaphysics*

There is a distinction in the judgments we make about things. Some judgments add nothing to what we already know. Others increase our knowledge. The former are called analytic judgments; the latter, which increase our knowledge, are synthetic. Analytical judgments express nothing in the predicate but what has been already actually thought in the subject. When I say, "All bodies are extended in space," I have not increased my concept of body. I have only analyzed it. Occupying space was already part of the concept of a body before the judgment was made. It is only that it may not have been expressed explicitly and clearly. On the other hand, "All bodies have weight," is different. It contains the notion of weight, which is not actually thought in the general concept of body. It must therefore be called synthetic.

All analytical judgments depend entirely on logic and, in particular on the law of non-contradiction. Therefore, they are independent of and prior to any further experience. They are called *a priori* judgments. This is true whether the particular concepts in them come from experience or not, for the predicate of an analytical judgment is already contained in the subject. To deny the predicate of the subject would be a contradiction. For this reason, all analytical judgments are *a priori*, even if the concepts originally came from experience. For example, consider the sentence, "Gold is a yellow metal." For me to know this requires no additional experience, because my concept of "gold" already includes that it is "a yellow metal". I need only analyze the concept "gold" to make this judgment.

Synthetic judgments require more than logic. In addition to analytic judgments *a priori*, there are others that depend on and therefore come after some experience. These we call *a posteriori*. They are always synthetic, since it is our experience that enables us to make the judgment. But there are some synthetic judgments that are prior to, or independent of, experience. That is, they are synthetic *a priori*. They come entirely from our reason and understanding, yet there is *more* in the predicate than can be found by analyzing the subject purely by means of logic. That such judgments exist will become clear when we consider mathematical judgments, which we claim are both *a priori* and synthetic.

This fact about mathematics has escaped the notice of everyone who has thought about human reason. In fact, it seems directly opposed to all their opinions. Because mathematical truths are necessary and universal, people realized they could not be derived from particular experiences. They were therefore recognized as *a priori*. However, since mathematical proofs depend only on logic, people persuaded themselves that the fundamental principles – the axioms or postulates – were also known that way. This was a great mistake. A synthetic proposition can indeed be proved by logic but only by presupposing another synthetic statement, a postulate, from which it follows. This postulate in turn, however, requires more than logic to establish its truth.

At first, one might think that the proposition 7 + 5 = 12 is analytic and follows by logic from the sum of 7 + 5. but closer examination shows that this is an error. The thought of the sum of 7+5 contains merely their union in a single number. It does not contain the particular number, 12, that unites them. We can analyze this sum "7 + 5", as much as we want, we will never find the "12" in it. We must call to our aid an image, or intuition, that corresponds to one of the concepts. This can happen by means of our imaginations or experience, though this experience is only the occasion for the emergence of the image. For example, we must utilize our five fingers to correspond to the concept 5. Then we must necessarily add the units in the image to the concept 7 to create the new concepts of 8,9,10,11 and finally 12. Hence our concept of "7 + 5" is really extended by the proposition "7 + 5 = 12." We must join to the concept "7 + 5", a new concept "12", which was not thought in it. Arithmetical judgments are therefore all synthetic. This is even clearer if we take much larger numbers. For in such cases it is obvious that however much we analyze our concepts by logic we would never find the sum.

The axioms and postulates of geometry are also synthetic. For example, "a straight line is the shortest distance between two points," is a synthetic truth. My idea of straight does not contain anything about quantity, but only about the quality of the line, its straightness. The concept of the quantity "shortest" is therefore entirely an addition. Logic cannot extract it from the concept "straight line". The ambiguity of our expressions about mathematics is what confuses us. We say that a given concept like "shortest" *must* be attached to a concept like "straight line". That is agreed. But the question is not what our thinking is forced to join to a given concept, but *how* it is forced. Is it by logic that we extract what is already only vaguely in our thought? Or must we look to an image in our imaginations to feel the necessity of joining the concepts together?

88

Questions

1.   Is there a difference between "7 + 5 = 12" and "A straight line is the shortest distance between two points" in terms of:

	Same	Different
a). Their relation to experience.		
b). How true each one is.		
c). How certain you are about their truth.		
d). How well they exemplify Kant's claim.		

2.   Is there anything at all that might shake your belief in the truth of either of the examples in #1?

Why or why not?

3.   Three possible characteristics of mathematics were mentioned: a) We can agree on mathematics. b) Mathematical truths are often not obvious. c) Future experience will not change our minds about these truths.

Do you agree with all of them?

How would you order these characteristics in regard to how strongly you think they are true of mathematics?

XI

BEYOND THE IMAGINATION
TEXT: Lobachevski, *Theory of Parallels*

Orientation:

The imagination is perhaps the most curious power of the human mind. It appears to be a hybrid or cross between sensation and thinking, or reasoning. When we sense something, when we see or taste or touch it, the object is there close at hand in roughly the same place where we are. In contrast, when we think, our minds are freed from everything we have ever seen or sensed, from what is nearby or far off, from what exists or, as some claim, even can exist. Imagination is both similar to and distinct from these activities. Like thinking, what we imagine is not present to us – either close by or far off. Like seeing, imagining usually has a visual aspect, though if what we imagine really were visible, it would no longer be imagined but actually seen. Because imagination is a blend of these other two powers, it has often functioned as a bridge between the particular objects we sense, experience and remember, and the classes or groups of objects – all triangles, all animals – which we often think about. In addition, it has been crucial in poetry, painting, fiction, and mathematics (especially in geometry), as a tool for exploration and discovery. For these subjects, it has functioned as a kind of experiment whose results we attempt to reconfirm through sensation, action, or thinking. Many athletes have reported that visualizing or imagining a particular movement or event has played an important part in perfecting it. Many scientists and mathematicians have first imagined what they later discovered and demonstrated.

When we imagine something in great detail, though we may not be sure whether it actually exists or is merely imaginary, we at least feel confident that it is not contradictory, or completely impossible. Many accounts of imagination claim that the elements or building blocks we use come from what we have seen or experienced, but that these elements are combined by free creations of the mind. A good example is in science fiction. Though writers have imagined the strangest creatures from other galaxies and other dimensions, the elements or components of these beings are nonetheless recognizable. Imagination presents us with a possible situation which may be shown to have features in common with our own experiences. Examples of products of the imagination abound in the films and novels we confront. Though we recognize that films and fiction are often different in important aspects from our daily

---

Nikolai Ivanovich Lobachevski (1793-1856) was born in Makariev, Russia. He was educated at the University of Kazan, where he became Professor of Mathematics in 1816. He became the head of the University in 1827, two years before he published his work on geometry. It was only after his death that the revolutionary significance of his work was recognized.

experience, we nonetheless can learn things from them.

In this unit, we will investigate what happens in geometry or in mathematics when the imagination can no longer be used. We stated that what we can imagine is, at least, not completely impossible. What happens, however, when we reverse this situation? When we can't imagine something, does that mean that what we claim is in fact impossible? This situation occurs in the text by Lobachevski, which will present his revolutionary view of parallel lines. Is his position absurd because it conflicts with our imaginations? If his position is not absurd, can imagination still play some role in this form of mathematics? Or is it that imagination misleads us, and that mathematics must be independent of imagination, diagrams, and visual examples?

Lobachevski takes one of the decisive steps in mathematics by helping to create non-Euclidean geometry, which denies the Euclidian claim about parallelism. His work does not solve some particular problem, but rather consists in presenting a new view of parallel lines. In Euclidean geometry, through a point not on a particular line, only one line can be constructed parallel to that specific line. In contrast to this, Lobachevski claims that through a point *more than one line* could be constructed parallel to a specific line.

Lobachevski's claim raises a series of questions about which people still disagree. Some of these questions concern the nature of mathematical objects, some concern the process of doing geometry, and some concern the goals of geometry. Lobachevski's work raises questions about the nature of the lines and figures we construct when we do geometry and about the roles that intuition and imagination play in mathematics. It forces us to ask what it means to say that a mathematical theory is true and how we should decide between incompatible theories. Is deciding between conflicting views of parallel lines like deciding between two theories in science? Or, is it more like choosing between two desirable meals to eat for dinner? These are some of the issues that arise from Lobachevski's investigations. In this unit we will consider his approach in the theorem that presents his ideas about parallel lines.

In Euclid's geometry, parallel lines are treated in a way that appears obvious to most of us and captures how most people claim they imagine straight lines. If we consider a line CD and a point off that line, A, through that point only one line AB will be parallel to the initial line in a given plane.

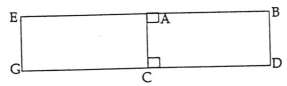

There are a number of ways to visualize this claim. One way is to drop a perpendicular from the point A to the line CD, forming a right angle at C. Then, the angle CAB will also be a right angle. This is how we construct the Euclidian parallel to CD. This line will remain the parallel if extended in the direction of E as the line BAE. It will also remain equidistant from CD. The lines EG, AC, and BD are all equal. In other words, the line BAE never gets closer or farther away from the line CD, and this model can be repeated for any other point, say F. There are two characteristics of these parallel lines. *They don't intersect or cut one another,* and *they remain at the same distance.* It is certainly clear that if the lines remain at the same distance, they don't cut one another. But what about the reverse? How do we know that straight lines do cut each other if they continuously get closer and closer? Our imaginations seem to force us to say they will cut, but why should we *always* trust our imagination? Do we *know* they will cut? Lobachevski breaks this connection between the idea of lines that do not intersect and their equidistance. To do this he will make a distinction between two concepts that we usually identify with one another: that of parallel lines and that of lines that do not intersect. If you read Unit III on Metaphors in Mathematics, this step is similar to the approach explored in regard to the finite and infinite.

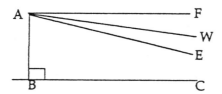

The key concept for Lobachevski is the non-cutting line. He claims that through a point A more than one non-cutting line in a given plane can be constructed to line BC. AE, AF, and AW would be three such lines. In addition, once one has more than one such non-cutting line through the point A (for example, the two non-cutting lines AE and AW) then all the infinitely many other lines through point A that lie between AE and AW must also be non-cutting lines with respect to the line BC. Lobachevski envisions such an infinite collection of lines through any point in respect to a given line. He then defines the parallel as *the last such non-cutting line,* AE. In Euclidian geometry there is only one line through a point which does not cut a given line. This line is also the parallel. Since there is no difference between the parallel line and the non-cutting line, the parallel does not have to be defined in a manner similar to what Lobachevski does. The parallel line is therefore the central concept. For Lobachevski, the identity is broken and the priority reversed– the central concept appears to be the non-cutting line. Does this claim, that there is more than one non-cutting line, conflict with our geometrical intuitions, or with our sense of space, or with what we feel we know about straight lines through our imaginations? If it does, should these intuitions or images play a role in mathematics, and what are these intuitions? Where do we get them? Are we born with them? Do we learn them from our experience? Do we develop them within our culture and could we learn to develop new intuitions – Lobechevskian ones?

One must explore whether anything in our experience conforms to Lobachevski's approach. For example, we know that railway tracks must remain at the same distance from one another at each point in order for the train not to be derailed. Imagine standing in the middle of the tracks and looking down at them in either direction. The rails will appear to converge. They will appear to us to get closer and closer even though we *know* that the rails can never meet. For many centuries, artists have utilized this fact of perspective. Whenever they draw parallel lines, they make them converge to make them look as if they are getting farther and farther away from us. So even if we assume that the world we live in is Euclidian, we must admit that the way we often see that world is non-Euclidian. One might therefore say that some of our visual experience is non-Euclidian, or in fact partially Lobachevskian.

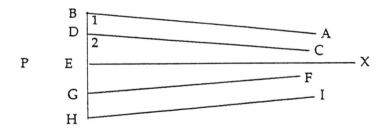

If the railway tracks were wider apart or closer together, or in general if the Euclidian parallels we wished to represent in perspective were farther apart or closer to one another, we would see them converge at different rates. The manner of their convergence – the angles of convergence, angles ABE, and CDE – would differ from one another. If we stood at point P, halfway between the two sets of railroad tracks and looked towards X, the angles at 1 and 2 would be different. This fact about angles is a further consequence of Lobachevskian geometry. The farther a point is from the line to which one is drawing a parallel, the smaller the angle of the last non-cutting line – that is, the parallel. The closer the point gets, the larger the angle. In other words, angle CDE is greater than angle ABE. The farther out the point is along the perpendicular BE through it to the line XE, the smaller the angle.

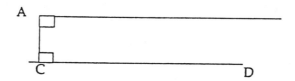

This is another great difference between this geometry and Euclid's, where the perpendicular distance AC of the point A from the line CD to which a parallel is drawn is irrelevant to the angle formed at A. It is always a right angle. Lobachevski captures this difference in his theorem by saying that the angle of parallelism is a function of distance, or f(x) = angle of parallelism, where x is the perpendicular distance from the point to the line.

What should one think about Lobachevski's explorations? Can we call it a geometry, or is it just a mental exercise that we should not consider to be of the same status as Euclidian geometry? Does the fact that we actually experience visually some of the crucial aspects of Lobachevski's theorem show that these unusual claims about straight lines are at least possible and not absurd? Would using this geometry or growing up with it in school perhaps even lead to a new type of imagining? Or is Lobachevski's geometry really absurd if it is supposed to be about geometrical straight lines and not just the visual lines we see? If, for the moment, we grant that Lobachevski's geometry is not absurd in the sense that it is entirely self-consistent — that is, if we follow only his rules, we never contradict ourselves — would anything convince you that it, rather than Euclidean geometry, is true? Or could they both be true? If you think they could both be true, what do you mean by true? Or is this possibility also absurd, and must we choose one or the other?

TEXT

Lobachevski: *The Theory of Parallels*

All the straight lines in a plane that go out from a point can, with reference to a given straight line in the same plane, be divided into two classes: into those that cut that line and those that don't.

The boundary lines of the one and the other class of these lines will be called parallel to the given line.

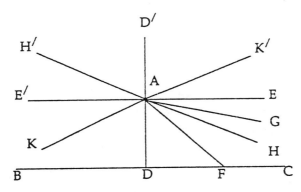

From the point A, let fall upon the line BC the perpendicular AD, to which again draw the perpendicular AE.

In the right angle EAD either all the straight lines which go out from the point A meet the line DC, as for example AF, or some of them, like the perpendicular AE, will not meet the line DC. In the uncertainty, whether the perpendicular AE is the only line that does not meet DC, we will assume it may be possible that there are still other lines, for example AG, which do not cut DC, how far soever they may be prolonged. In passing over from the cutting lines, as AF, to the non-cutting line is a boundary line, upon one side of which all lines AG are such as do not meet the line DC, while upon the other side every straight line AF cuts the line DC.

The angle HAD between the parallel HA and the perpendicular AD is called the parallel angle (or the angle of parallelism), which we will here designate by f(p), for AD=p. If f(p) is a right angle, so will the prolongation AE of the perpendicular AE likewise be parallel to the prolongation DB of the line DC. In addition, we remark that in regard to the four right angles, which are made at the point A by the perpendiculars AE and AD, and their prolongations AE and AD, every straight line that goes out from the point A, either itself or at least its prolongation, lies in one of the two right angles that are turned toward BC. So that, except the parallel EE, all others, if they are sufficiently produced both ways, must intersect the line BC.

If the angle of parallelism is less than 90°, in other words, if f(p) <90°, then upon the other side of AD, making the same angle DAK = f(p), is a line AK parallel to the prolongation DB of the line DC. So that under this assumption we must also make a distinction of sides in parallelism.

All remaining lines, or their prolongations, within the two right angles turned toward BC pertain to those that intersect, if they lie within the angle HAK = 2 f(p) between the parallels. They pertain on the other hand to the non-intersecting AG, if they lie upon the other sides of the parallels AH and AK, in the opening of the two angles EAH = 90 - f(p), E AK =90-f(p), between the parallels and EE the line which is perpendicular to AD. Upon the other side of the perpendicular, EE, the prolongations AH and AK of the parallels AH and AK will likewise be parallel to BC. The remaining lines, belong, if in the angle K AH, to the class of intersecting lines, but if in the angles K AE, H AE to the non-intersecting lines.

In accordance with this approach, for the assumption f(p) =<90°, the lines can be only intersecting or parallel. but if we assume that f(p) <90°, then we must allow two parallels, one on the one and one on the other side. In addition, we must distinguish the remaining lines into non-intersecting and intersecting.

For both assumptions it serves as the mark of parallelism that the lines between the parallel and the given line become intersecting for the smallest angular deviation. This means if AH is parallel to DC, every line AF cuts DC, how small soever the angle HAF may be.

Questions

After Lobachevski, a number of other mathematicians attempted to create variant geometries by denying one or more Euclidian postulates. Listed below (a-e) are some of these attempts. Which Euclidian postulates are denied by each of these suggestions or by their consequences? They may deny one or more or none.

a. All straight lines intersect - i.e., there are no parallel lines.
b. Two straight lines can enclose a space - that is, form a close figure.
c. All straight lines are finite.
d. Straight lines that are extended far enough return to their origin and begin to coincide with themselves.
e. Three points determine a unique straight line - between any two points, more than one straight line exists.

Euclidian Postulates

Let the following be postulated:
1. It is possible to draw a straight line from any point to any point.
2. It is possible to produce a finite straight line continuously in a straight line.
3. It is possible to describe a circle with any center and distance.
4. All right angles are equal to one another.
5. If a straight line falling on two straight lines makes the interior angles on the same side less than two right angles, then the two straight lines, if produced indefinitely, meet on the side on which the angles are less than two right angles.

Lobachevski gives a diagram. Does that help or not? Are there any improvements or suggestions you could make about the diagram that would help others grasp the central ideas?

XII	IT'S AXIOMATIC
	TEXT: Hilbert, *The Foundations of Geometry*

Orientation:

Buildings, bridges, and other architectural structures have foundations. Engineers and our own experience, sometimes unfortunate, tell us that these structures can only be as strong as what they are built on. If the foundation is weak or flawed, the structure collapses. This image has found a home in many subjects: the sciences, morality, and, in particular, mathematics. It is important, however, to ask why this image is so captivating. Why do we feel that we are more comfortable with certain subjects or topics when we possess or can describe their foundations? Is it because we feel that we have reduced something complex into its simple components, which are easier to understand? Is it because we feel more certain, or sure of ourselves, when we can build up or prove one claim from another even if we realize we must ultimately accept certain claims without proof? Is it because we find it easier to explain to someone else, or to ourselves why we believe or do something when we can present what it depends on or what supports it? All or some of these considerations may be involved.

Whatever the reason, the image of a foundation is not the only one we could use. For example, the image of a jigsaw puzzle would take us in a different direction from the image of a foundation. In a jigsaw puzzle, there is no foundation. Instead, the parts are all equal in status, and the whole emerges from the proper arrangement of the pieces. Is this image appropriate for mathematics? If not for mathematics, which subjects or activities are best characterized in this way?

Hilbert was the central thinker in developing the image of a foundation for mathematics. His axioms for Euclidian geometry are intended as a foundation for that subject matter. He claims that axioms result from a logical analysis of our intuition of space. In other words, if we analyze logically our intuitive sense of space, we will find a set of claims that explicitly state what we assume or believe or know when we think about geometrical figures and do geometry.

One simple example will reveal the direction such an analysis would take. Elementary geometry deals with *points* and *lines* in a *plane*. These three different geometrical objects do not exist independently of one another but are interrelated.

David Hilbert (1862-1943) was born in Königsberg, Germany. He became Professor of Mathematics first at Königsberg and later at Gottingen. He worked in many fields of mathematics, including the theory of numbers, geometry, and set theory. His principal efforts, however, were investigating the presuppositions of mathematical proof and the structure of mathematical systems. Hilbert's work set the stage for all modern discussions of the nature of mathematics.

How many points are needed uniquely to determine a straight line? If we have a straight line, does that straight line have points on it? If so, how many points do we know about? If we have a straight line, and we know that two points on it are in a specific plane, then, if the straight line has other points, are those points in the same plane or in a different one? These are examples of very general questions one might ask about the relations among the three elements – *point, line, plane* – of geometry.

Hilbert believes that an answer to each question of this kind produces an axiom. Hilbert states approximately 40 axioms. He believes, in short, that everything we require to prove a theorem in geometry must be stated. Often when we are doing geometry, we refer to a diagram or to a vague feeling or mental image that we have of lines and points, figures, and their interrelation. For Hilbert, all these vague feelings must be stated clearly. Hilbert believes that in mathematics nothing should go without saying, and nothing is supposed to be too obvious to mention. A complete list of these most basic statements would supply the foundation for geometry.

Such a goal may seem desirable to us. Often in arguments and disagreements and even in discussions where there is no conflict, a great deal goes without saying. Sometimes we find ourselves retracing the same ground over and over again without making any progress. Not infrequently the reason for such an impasse is that what is really at issue has remained concealed from all the participants. In this type of case, one often feels frustrated and wishes that someone would make explicit what is really at stake. There are, however, many other cases where intellectual exploration or a successful action occurs precisely because not every "t" was crossed and not every "i" dotted. Imagine what would happen if all our assumptions and presuppositions had to be made explicit before we could undertake anything. Wouldn't our situation be similar to the one the character Hamlet has come to represent – a paralysis caused by excessive thought? Hilbert chooses this first option. Does this strike you as an appropriate goal in general or only in mathematics? If it is important in mathematics, why is this subject matter one which requires it? And do you believe it is possible to state everything that is needed in order to prove a mathematical theorem?

When we decide to attempt to make everything explicit, it seems tempting to begin with definitions. However, Hilbert surprisingly does not take this obvious route. Unlike Euclid, Hilbert does not define any of the crucial objects or elements of the geometry – for example, points or lines. If your class did the lesson on definitions, Unit I, you will remember that Euclid defined a point as *that which has no part*, and a straight line as *a line that lies evenly with the points on itself*. These definitions do not in any normal sense enable us to explain what points and lines are to someone who doesn't already know what they are. Nor does Euclid ever refer to these definitions in any of his proofs. Nonetheless, they seem to play some role in the way Euclid conceives of mathematics.

Hilbert's conception must be radically different, even though he seems to focus on the same subject matter. Hilbert says no more about points and lines than that they are distinct from one another and will be referred to by different kinds of letters: upper case letter for points, lower case for lines. Since we have no definitions, the axioms must contain everything we need to know about these objects. The information we would learn from such axioms, however, is different from what we would gain from definitions. Definitions often attempt to state _what_ an object is. Axioms generally describe relations between objects. So, without definitions the axioms could be true of a variety of objects. The first axiom, _that two distinct points, A and B, uniquely determine a straight line a,_ really states that two distinct elements of one kind, viz., points, uniquely determine an element of the other kind, viz., a straight line. In a system of geometry without parallel lines - that is, one in which all straight lines intersect - Hilbert's first axiom would be reciprocally true of lines and points. In other words, we could exchange the words 'lines' and 'points' and the axiom would still hold. Without parallel lines, any two straight lines intersect only once and therefore uniquely determine a point. If the elements of a system of geometry are entirely determined by the axioms - if we did not have definitions - there would be no way to tell the difference between points and lines. Does this strike you as a problem or as an advantage?

Hilbert believes that axioms for geometry must satisfy three criteria. They must be _simple, complete,_ and _independent._ The characteristics of completeness and independence are easier to describe than the simplicity. _Independence_ means that no axiom can be proved from the other axioms, either singly or in combination. Any axiom that we could prove from other axioms would become a theorem. Since, however, theorems as well as axioms can be used to prove new theorems, we would end up with the same set of truths. _Completeness,_ the second criterion, deals with the collection of statements, theorems, that we can prove from the axioms. There is a large collection of statements in Euclidian plane geometry that we consider true. Examples are: _the base angles of isosceles triangles are equal, the angle sum of a triangle is equal to two right angles,_ the Pythagorean Theorem, and many others. That is, there are many geometrical statements that we believe so strongly to be true that we want, we insist, that they be included in any complete system of Euclidian geometry. If some of these could not be proved from our axioms, the system would be incomplete. We would then need to add axioms. The third criterion, _simplicity,_ is harder to describe. It should be considered when his axioms are discussed in class.

Though Hilbert presents many axioms, approximately 40, they fall into five major groups. Presumably, the groups present for him the places where there is a real separation among the axioms. The groups are called 1) Axioms of Connection,

2) Axioms of Order, 3) Axioms of Parallelism, 4) Axioms of Congruence, and 5)Axioms of Continuity. They represent Hilbert's way of giving an account of the crucial aspects of geometry. Our text will present only his first two groups: Axioms of Connection and of Order. These will reveal the direction and turn of his work. Connection axioms answer the kinds of questions raised earlier about points and lines: namely, how they are connected with one another. Order axioms tell us how points are ordered. As Hilbert says, they describe the use of the word "between". The Axioms of Parallelism tells us when lines intersect and when they don't. Lines which intersect can form figures that may be identical or not. These form the topic of the fourth group of axioms – the Axioms of Congruence. The fifth group completes Hilbert's version of Euclidian geometry by stating the conditions under which lines are continuous – the Axioms of Continuity.

We probably assume that the continuity of lines is one of the first aspects of our intuition, whereas Hilbert lists it at the end. This becomes an issue to consider because, as you will see, Hilbert states theorems after each set of axioms that can be proved just by those specific axioms. After the first axiom group, he states the theorem, *Two straight lines of a plane have either one point or no point in common.* This theorem is to be proved using only the axioms of connection. After the second axiom group, he states the theorem, *Between any two points of a straight line, there always exists an unlimited number of points.* In the questions, you are asked to create such a proof. We must keep in mind that at this stage of Hilbert's development of the foundations we do not know if the lines we are considering are continuous or not. Since this claim about the number of points on straight lines is a theorem, the axioms used to prove it must be what Hilbert considers simpler. Do you agree with him, or would you rather assume this theorem as an axiom? What is his idea of simplicity? Since his groups of axioms seem to build on one another while bringing up new aspects of geometry, a question arises: What is the best image to describe how the axioms are a foundation? If you read Euclid's postulates either in Unit V or in the questions to Unit XI, you might consider if those also build on one another. Is the image of the foundation of a building helpful? Does that image need to be modified? For example, are the axioms of connection also, in some sense, a foundation for the axioms of order since the first group is required to state the second group?

TEXT

Hilbert: *Foundations of Geometry*

Geometry, like arithmetic, requires for its logical development only a small number of simple, fundamental principles. These fundamental principles are called the axioms of geometry. The choice of the axioms and the investigation of their relations to one another is a problem that, since the time of Euclid, has been discussed in numerous excellent memoirs to be found in the mathematical literature. This problem is tantamount to the logical analysis of our intuition of space.

The following investigation is an attempt to choose for Euclidian geometry a *simple and complete set of independent* axioms and to deduce from these the most important geometrical theorems. These proofs are to be done in such a manner as to bring out as clearly as possible the significance of the different groups of axioms and the scope of the conclusions to be derived from the individual axioms.

I. The Elements of Geometry and the Five Groups of Axioms

Let us consider three distinct systems of things. The things composing the first system we will call points, and designate them by the letters A,B,C,...; those of the second, we will call straight lines, and designate them by the letters a,b,c,...; and those of the third system, we will call *planes* and designate them by the Greek letters α, β, γ.

Points are called the *elements of linear geometry;* the points and straight lines, the *elements of plane geometry;* and the points, lines, and planes, the *elements of geometry of space* or the *elements of space.*

We think of these points, straight lines, and planes as having certain mutual relations, which we indicate by means of such words as "are situated", "between", "parallel", "congruent", "continuous", etc. The complete and exact description of these relations follows as a consequence of the *axioms of geometry.* These axioms may be arranged in five groups. Each of these groups expresses, by itself, certain related fundamental facts of our intuition. We will name these groups as follows:

I.   Axioms of *connection*
II.   Axioms of *order*
III.   Axioms of *parallels*
IV.   Axioms of *congruence*
V.   Axioms of *continuity*

GROUP I. AXIOMS OF CONNECTION

The axioms of this group establish a connection between the concepts indicated above: namely, points and straight lines. These axioms are as follows:

I,1. *Two distinct points A and B always completely determine a straight line a. We write AB = a or BA = a*

Instead of "determine", we may also employ other forms of expression; for example, we may say *A* "lies upon" *a*, *A* "is a point on "*a*, *a* "goes through" *A* "and through" *B*, *a* "joins" *A* "and" or "with" *B*, etc.

I,2. *Any two distinct points of a straight line completely determine that line; that is, if AB =a and AC =a, where B is a different point from C, then is also BC = a.*

THEOREM 1. Two straight lines of a plane have either one point or no point in common.

GROUP II. AXIOMS OF ORDER

The axioms of this group define the idea expressed by the word "between," and make possible, upon the basis of this idea, an *order of sequence* of the points upon a straight line.   The points of a straight line have a certain relation to one another which the word "between" serves to describe. The axioms of this group are as follows:

II, 1. *If A,B,C, are points of a straight line and B lies between A and C, then B lies also between C and A.*

II, 2. *If A and C are two points of a straight line, then there exists at least one point B lying between A and C and at least one point D so situated that C lies between A and D.*

II, 3. *Of any three points situated on a straight line, there is always one and only one that lies between the other two.*

II, 4. *Any four points, A,B,C,D of a straight line can always be so arranged that B shall lie between A and C and also between A and D, and furthermore, that C shall lie between A and D and also between B and D.*

Axioms II, 1-4 contain statements concerning the points of a straight line only, and hence, we will call them the *linear axioms of group II.*

CONSEQUENCES OF THE AXIOMS OF CONNECTION AND ORDER

By the aid of the preceding axioms we can deduce the following theorem:

THEOREM 2. Between any two points of a straight line, there always exists an unlimited number of points.

Questions

1. Write out a proof for Hilbert's theorem #2.

2. Unlike Euclid, Hilbert gives no definitions of point and line. Do you find that a problem or an improvement? Which of the reasons below do you think is more acceptable in explaining why one should avoid giving definitions?

   a) Definitions of point and line cannot be given.

   b) A definition would encourage us to use a picture or image.

3. Do you think everything needed for a proof in geometry can be clearly and explicitly stated? Why or why not?

XIII

MATHEMATICAL PHYSICS AND PHYSICAL MATHEMATICS

TEXT: Newton, *Mathematical Principles of Natural Philosophy*

Orientation:

In high school and college, mathematics and physics are studied as two completely different subjects. Students have different teachers for these subjects, and they are members of distinct high school and college departments. According to the way we currently structure what we know, these subjects are different. This division of labor is taken even farther. Within each of these subjects, there is extensive specialization. A person is not simply a mathematician or physicist, but concentrates on an even more specialized sub-field, e.g., set theory or topology in mathematics, and plasma or solid state physics. Within each subject, there is also another type of distinction. Some are pure mathematicians, others do applied mathematics; in physics, some are experimenters, others are theoreticians.

Pure mathematicians generally explore and create mathematical systems with no concern about any possible use. Applied mathematicians often particularize these results to deal with concrete problems in science or in specialized mathematical fields. This latter group sometimes interacts with theoretical physicists, who suggest theoretical constructs for the data supplied by experimenters. This neat division of tasks, however, only works when a field of study is stable and already definite in its outlines. In periods of great ferment, as is now occurring in chaos theory, the divisions crumble. Some of the mathematics of chaos theory was developed by physicists, while mathematicians are using computers as experimental devices to generate new data to verify their theorems. This phenomenon hearkens back to the period beginning about the mid-17th century and lasting into the late 18th century, when our present structure of knowledge took shape. The current division between physics and mathematics may continue, or we may in the future find it more useful either to adapt the previous model in which these subjects were not separate or to turn to some third option.

In this unit, we will consider whether mathematics and physics should be one subject or two. We will do this by considering the work of a thinker who occupies

Isaac Newton (1642-1727) was born in Lincolnshire, England. He was educated at Cambridge, where he became Professor of Mathematics. Creator of the calculus, the theory of gravitation, and the theory of light as a mixture of colors, his work set the direction for science for the next two centuries. In 1687 he published *Mathematical Principles of Natural Philosophy,* considered by many to be the most influential work ever written.

a focal place in both the history of mathematics, for the calculus, and in the history of physics, for the theory of gravitation. Newton was neither a mathematician nor a physicist, however, but was instead a fusion of the two. His approach will enable us to consider the general question of the costs and gains of specialization and the costs and gains of obscuring the boundaries between subjects. This question does not only affect work in mathematics and physics but influences us at every moment of our lives. Newton's work is a kind of case study of this issue.

Prior to Newton, the relation between mathematics, which was primarily geometry, and the study of nature or physics was entirely ambiguous. Some people like Galileo and Descartes felt that geometry was applicable or was even the key to the whole study of nature. Others felt that no two subjects could be more different, because mathematics concerns what does not change, while nature presents us with a variety of continual changes: change of place, growth, alteration, birth and death, increase and decrease, and many others. To view nature geometrically, they thought, would be both to strip it of what made nature natural, and to re-immerse mathematics into the very realm of experience from which 2000 years of fertile thinking had freed it.

This is the impasse Newton faced. His response was to reconstrue both mathematics and nature. Following a few previous thinkers, he focused on what he considered the most general type of motion – change of place – and subordinated all the other changes to it. He confronted previous mathematics, which, along with philosophy, was stymied by the issue of describing or defining change and motion, and he raised a question mathematicians had not asked, namely, whether the types of motion can be subordinated under one general type. This question would seem inappropriate for a mathematician, for they dealt with unchanging entities. Geometers proved theorems about straight lines, curves, and such figures. Therefore, by asking this question about motion, Newton was viewing mathematics as a student of nature, or as a physicist, would. Furthermore, previous thinkers about nature attempted to respect and catalogue the details and differences they observed in motion. Though some attempted a definition of motion, they rarely asked whether there is one type of motion of which the others are merely special cases. Newton generalized all changes as dependent on one principal type of motion – change of place. By taking this step, he viewed nature as a mathematician might.

By obscuring the boundary between these subject matters, Newton created an entirely new subject that he called the Mathematical Principles of Natural Philosophy. ("Natural Philosophy" is the name given to what we now call "Physics".) This special perspective of Newton does not presently exist as a subject matter. The subject was split apart, and again roughly follows the pre-Newtonian divisions into mathematics and physics – though of course with an entirely different and post-Newtonian content.

The mathematics is now called the calculus; the physics he created is now known as Newtonian mechanics and the theory of gravitation. This unit's reading will contain excerpts from Newton's text. These passages will show the outlines of his perspective.

The first reading is from the Preface of his book. This is where Newton attempts to remove the boundaries between mathematics and mechanics, or physics. The previous distinction focused on the fact that, in mathematics, demonstrations are possible in which we achieve certainty, whereas in mechanics, one always has more or less success in building machines and describing the movements of objects. On the one hand, our drawings and constructions never achieved a geometrical precision resulting in perfectly straight lines, and on the other hand, actual physical motions are always somewhat irregular in path and duration. Most thinkers had considered these as essential differences between the two subjects. Newton does not. The difference for him is not in the subject matters – the arts as he calls them – but in the artisans. Some "artisans" might be able to draw perfect lines, whereas we humans can't. Focusing on the lines, he asks his crucial questions. *Where do the lines we study come from?* and, *How are they generated or drawn?* Since these questions concern motion, they make mathematics a branch of mechanics. The difference between mathematics and physics is no longer a contrast between the eternal and the changing, but between the more or less precise. Newton's answer to his questions is found in the second passage in the reading, his First Law of Motion.

Newton's first law is enshrined in every physics book written from the time he first enunciated it in 1687 until now, and will possibly never be replaced. From the point of view of the current subject matter called physics, it states that there is no difference between a body at rest and one at constant speed in a straight line. A physical explanation or cause, in the form of the action of some *other* body, is required to explain a *change* of speed or a *change* of direction. That is, we don't need to explain a body at rest or in constant motion in a straight line, but we must explain *change*, whether that is in the form of acceleration or of deceleration, or of a curved path of motion.

From Newton's perspective, however, his first law asserts what draws and generates the straight lines. The movement of each object, when it is not influenced by any other, generates perfect straight lines. Of course, we never experience these lines. In Newton's theory of universal gravitation, at every moment every object in the universe always attracts every other body, irrespective of their distance from one another. What we see are at most only approximately straight lines, which are more or less curved. This occurs because what we actually see is the composite of an object moving according to Law 1, together with changes caused by the attraction of every other object. We are told by Law 2 in the reading that this change also occurs along a perfect straight line. Since, however, every other object in the universe attracts this specific object along the straight lines that connect it and each of the others, the result is a straight line that is a composite of all these movements. This is spelled out in Corollary 1 in the reading. But the slightest movement by the particular object we are focusing on results in a different tiny composite straight line. The result which we experience will therefore look like a curve. A perfect straight line would be visible to us only if there were just one object in existence or if all the objects that exist did not continually attract one another, as in fact they do. Since neither situation describes our world, such straight lines are never visible. This does not, however, affect Newton's claim. This actual situation does not mean that straight lines *cannot* exist in our world as mathematicians previously held. It only means that we can never experience them. Underlying what we do see are the very tiny movements in perfect straight lines. We can't see them, but we might be able to *think* them if we can create a tool that enables us to describe the movement of the object from moment to moment.

The tool must describe these lines from moment to moment. This is because each object continually attracts every other. So just at the moment that a perfect straight line begins to be drawn, the object in a new position is, by attraction of all the objects, moved along a different straight line. So the straight lines are infinitesimal in length. Newton developed a tool to achieve the task of describing these motions. In Newton's work, the tool and what it is used for form a unity. It is a *physical mathematics.* Later the tool and its use were separated into a branch of mathematics called the calculus (the tool), which is utilized in a part of physics called Newtonian mechanics (its use). This latter is what we call mathematical physics.

As you read the Preface, the two laws, and Corollary 1, you should mark the words or expressions that strike you as coming from mathematics, and those which concern physics. What prompts you to choose one rather than the other? In other words, what do you believe is the main difference between mathematics and physics? Newton created a new form of thinking by removing the boundaries of two previously separate subjects. In your experience in school, which two subjects or topics would be better taught or understood if reconceived as one subject matter rather than two? This could be either because you feel one subject is really a part of the other, or that both are part of some third subject you feel you really should be studying. For example, do you think language arts and social studies should be taught as one subject or as two? This could be either the subject "humanities" or "world cultures". What are the gains and costs of this approach? What would it be like if English grammar and algebra were taught together? One way to get a handle on this issue is to ask yourself whether there is ever an issue that comes up in one of your courses that you would like to reexamine from the different perspective of another course.

TEXT

Newton: *Mathematical Principles of Natural Philosophy*

The ancient Greeks viewed science in two ways. One was called "rational" because it proceeds with complete accuracy by demonstration and proof. The other was practical. To practical science belonged all the engineering and building projects and the mechanical arts, using the five simple machines, such as the lever and pulley, which made these possible. These mechanical arts in fact gave mechanics its name. But as these workers do not work with complete accuracy, mechanics became distinguished from geometry, which considers perfectly accurate lines. These differences and errors in accuracy, however, are not part of the subject matters of geometry and mechanics. Rather, they are the result of the worker's skill or lack of it. He that works with less accuracy, he would be the most perfect mechanic of all. Such a perfect mechanic exists because the drawing and generation of straight lines and circles, upon which geometry is built, belongs to mechanics.

Geometry does not teach us how to draw straight lines and circles but requires that they be previously drawn. For geometry requires that the student should first be taught to draw these lines exactly before he can learn any geometry. Geometry itself shows how, by using straight lines and circles, many mathematical problems may be solved. Constructing straight lines and circles are problems, but they are not mathematical or geometrical problems. The solution of these problems therefore requires the science of mechanics. Once this is accomplished, geometry shows us how to use them. It is the glory of geometry that from those few principles, brought from mechanics, it is able to produce so many things. Therefore, geometry is founded on the mechanical practice of an absolutely perfect worker. Geometry is then truly merely a part of universal mechanics that demonstrates how to use lines, circles and various combinations of them to measure things and motions.

Law I

Every object continues in a state of rest or of uniform or constant speed in a straight line unless it is compelled to change that state of rest or constant speed in a straight line by external forces that act on it.

Projectiles continue their motions in a straight line so far as they are not slowed down by air resistance or drawn downward by the force of gravity. A top, whose parts by their cohesion are continually drawn aside from motion in a straight line and forced to rotate, only ceases its rotation through the retardation of the air. The planets and comets, meeting with less resistance in those freer spaces, continue their forward and curved or circular motions for a much longer time.

Law II

The change of motion in an object is proportional to the external force exerted on it. The change occurs along the straight line in which that force acts.

Force generates a motion. Twice that force will generate double the motion, three times that force will triple the motion. This happens whether the force is exerted on the object completely and at once, or gradually and successively. This motion is always generated in the same straight line as the action of the generating force. If the object changed was previously moving along the same straight line, the new motion is added to or subtracted from the former motion. Which it is depends on whether the force acts in the same or the opposite direction as the object was previously moving. If the new force acts along a straight line at some angle to the straight line motion of the object, the resulting motion will be along a third straight line, which is a compound of these two directions.

Corollary I

A body that is acted on by two forces simultaneously will trace out or draw the diagonal of a parallelogram in the same time it would trace out the sides of the parallelogram if acted on by those forces separately.

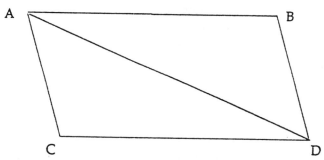

Assume that a body in place A has a force M impressed on it in a given time and because of this action moves with a uniform speed from A to B. Also assume that the same object in place A when acted on by a different force N alone would move from A to C. Construct a parallelogram ABCD. By both forces acting together on the object, it will in the same time move in the straight line along the diagonal from A to D. Force N acts in the direction of the line AC, which is parallel to BD. By the second law, this force N will not at all affect the direction or speed generated by the other force M, which moved the body toward the line BD. The body will therefore arrive in the same time somewhere along the line BD whether the force N acts or not. Therefore at the end of that time, it will be found somewhere on the line BD. By a similar argument, now viewed from the point of view of the effect of force M on the movement caused by force N toward C, the object will, at the end of the same time, also be somewhere along the line CD. It must therefore be at the point D, which is the only point both on lines BD and CD. But it will move in a straight line from A to D by Law 1. Therefore, it moves along the diagonal of the parallelogram ABCD, along the straight line AD.

Questions

1. Which two subjects would you most and least like to see combined into one course? #1 is most, and #7 is least. Rank the others between these extremes.

    1.— Music and Mathematics.
    2.— English Grammar and Algebra.
    3.— History and Literature.
    4.— Psychology and Literature.
    5.— Mathematics and Physics.
    6.— History and Government.
    7.— History and Mathematics.

    Explain your choice for #1.

    Explain your choice for #7.

2. Is Newton's first law true? How would one decide?

XIV

LEAPING TO THE UNIVERSAL
TEXTS: Poincaré, *Mathematical Induction;*
Mondrian, *Diamond Painting in Red, Yellow & Blue*

Orientation:

All our experience is of particular things. None of us has met all people, or played with or observed all dogs, or watched every object move, or added every number. Yet we all spend most of our time talking about groups of things or people, rather than about the specific objects we have seen and used. In fact, very few of us– primarily poets and artists – even have the ability to focus on and describe individuals in great detail. The rest of us talk and speak about many objects we have never directly experienced. The movement from the particular object we have seen, handled or met to those we haven't is generally imperceptible. This movement is called induction or generalization. Sometimes it is legitimate, at other times it is suspect. In this unit meeting, we will explore why we make this leap or jump from the particular to the general, and what role it plays in mathematics.

We will first consider how induction occurs in non-mathematical contexts and what its risks are. One risk is prejudice. All of us have heard Americans described as violent and greedy, and most of us have reacted strongly to such claims. Many of us feel that this remark is merely a prejudice. Some of us are violent and greedy, others aren't. Such a claim often has more to do with what the person making it wants to believe than with what the evidence warrants. We could assert in response that all Americans do not have any traits in common, or that, if they do, it is not these. Often the person who makes such a claim hasn't considered all the available evidence, either through neglect or indifference or for some other less neutral reason. Let us consider, however, another type of case. Suppose we do have all the available evidence and wish to take it all into account. There are still problems about induction. For example, what if we discovered that every time it rains in Bombay, the New York stock market rises. Would we begin to check the weather reports in India before investing money in New York? Presumably not. All the data we have agrees with this generalization, but we can't see how the data is evidence for it. The observations

Henri Poincaré (1854-1912) was born in Nancy, France. Educated in Paris, he became a professor of mathematics. He was one of the very few 20th century mathematicians who was also active in physics and astronomy as well as in almost all branches of mathematics. He was also unusual in his ability to write about highly technical matters in a way which was generally comprehensible.

Piet Mondrian (1872-1944) was born in Amersfoort, Holland. He worked in Paris from 1919-38 and at the outbreak of World War II went first to London and then New York. His abstract paintings in black, white, and primary colors have had a considerable influence on 20th century art.

seem like a strange coincidence, an accident. This is a second kind of risk. But there is a third kind we should consider. There are other cases that, unlike this one, don't seem accidental. Every one of our direct experiences shows that an object thrown into the air eventually falls to earth. For thousands of years, people believed this, however differently they tried to explain it. After Newton's theory of gravitation, however, people could envision an object thrown with enough velocity that it would never return. So a new theory supplied a different context for the evidence we had. It forced us to view our data as more limited than people imagined. In this case, certain details became more significant – like the velocity of the object thrown – and our conclusion became more limited, or less general. In other such cases, our conclusion could become more general.

There are therefore three major ways in which these inductive generalizations about experience can fail. First, the data can be limited as evidence because some has not been considered or because the group is an artificial creation. In the case of prejudice, either some evidence is not considered, or the group – Americans – is really only a creation of historians, sociologists, and politicians. The individuals we call Americans are really only members of the group of human beings. "Americans" is a name they have merely because of where they were born, grew up, or live. Second, the data – the rain in Bombay – isn't really evidence because it appears to be associated only by accident with the prices of stocks on the New York Exchange. Third, as in the case of thrown objects, a detail comes to take on more importance than we realized because of a new theory that forces us to reinterpret our data. This last case is always possible in such generalizations, and so even our best inductive conclusions about experience can always be reversed or modified. They are, to a certain extent, always tentative.

The case of mathematical induction is radically different from these. It is similar because we move from facts about particular numbers to claims about all the infinitely many numbers we haven't considered. However, unlike these other cases where even at best the conclusions are always tentative and open to revision, mathematical induction is a proof that equal in status to other proofs in mathematics is. In short, we will never be accused of prejudice in viewing only certain selected details, the claim will not be merely an accident or a coincidence, and we will never have to reverse ourselves. To explore these issues we will use two "texts". One is a painting, the other an example and a proposed explanation of this type of proof. The painting by Mondrian is a complete painting. Most viewers, however, have a vague sense that more exists beyond the canvas. In viewing the painting, we should consider what inclines us to suppose that what we see is only a part, or consider, more generally, what pushes us to go beyond what we have experienced to make claims about what we haven't experienced. The text by Poincaré presents mathematical

114

induction as the crucial feature of mathematical thinking, and explores how it differs from the induction we have just considered.

To examine Poincaré's claim, let us consider a mathematical instance that involves infinitely many numbers, but is similar to non-mathematical induction. Suppose we saw the first 10 terms in a series and they were 1,2,3,4,5,6,7,8,9,10,... What would come next? Probably most of us would say 11. Would we be shocked, however, if the next terms were 12,14,16,18,...? Probably we would be surprised, not shocked. We would simply claim we hadn't previously seen enough of this series. But how much is enough? Suppose it progresses by adding +2 up to 100. What happens then? Does it continue in this way? Have we seen enough then? Would it shock us if the series then continued 100,103,106,... or if it went 104,108,112,...? Each of these possibilities would give us a series with a definite rule, yet the rules are very different. In the first case we could propose the following rule. We begin the series with 10^0 (1) and go to 10^1 (10) by adding its exponent (1) to each number. From there to 10^2 (100) we add its exponent (2), and from there to 10^3 (1000) we add its exponent (3). In the second case the numbers added between 1 and 10, 10 and 100, 100 and 1000, would be determined according to the series 1,2,4,... . The two cases produce the same results by means of different rules up to 100, then diverge. As we get more data beyond 100, we can come to a decision between the rules. But this would not solve the problem. For in the second case, for example, we could ask ourselves what will happen beyond 1000. This depends on how we view the series 1,2,4,... Is the next number in the series 6 or 8? Is this a series of the even numbers or of the powers of 2? And if one of these possibilities were eliminated there are countless others, all of which would hold up to a certain point even if they might not hold beyond it. So, here in arithmetic, we have a situation where no observation is "accidental", each number is where it is according to a definite rule, but we will never get enough information to get the rule. This situation, though dealing with mathematics and induction, is not mathematical induction but identical to the previous cases of tentative generalizations.

In mathematical induction, the method of proof asserts that if we can show that a claim is true in two special cases, we will have shown it for all numbers. We first show by checking or substitution that a specific claim or property holds of the number "1". We then prove that *if* we assume that this claim or property holds for a specific number, represented by the letter "n", *then* it also holds for its successor, n+1. In other words, where n stands for any number, we prove that if it holds for n then it holds for the number n+1. The thrust of this remark is that we consider two successive numbers. These are variously described in proofs as n-1 and n, or as n and n+1. These are identical descriptions. These two steps, it is held, allow us to conclude that the claim is true of all numbers. For example, suppose we check that a claim is true of 1. Then suppose we show that, *if* it is true of n, it is true of n+1. But we showed it is true of 1, so therefore it is true of 2. But since it is true of 2, it is true of 3, and so on. In other words, we summarize the series of arguments by concluding that it is true of all numbers. This movement is a type of induction, and yet it is completely certain - a proof. The issue is, How is this possible? What is it about us, or about numbers, or about both of us, that brings this about? Proof by mathematical induction is also quite different from other proofs we use in mathematics, particularly in geometry. These other proofs occur purely by means of logic. We begin with certain premises - either axioms or theorems we have already proved – and reason from them to new theorems. A typical case would be:

The angle sum of all triangles is 180°. (previously proved theorem)

All right angles equal 90°. (axiom)

The angle sum of the other two angles of a right triangle is 90°. (newly proved theorem)

In such a proof we reason by means of syllogisms – two premises leading to a conclusion – or sets of syllogisms which are strung together. These proofs never move from the particular case to one which is more general. Some, as in the example, begin with truths about all right triangles and all right angles and conclude with a statement about all members of a class. In other cases, the conclusions are about some members of a class. In other words, unlike in mathematical induction, they move from general cases to other general cases, or from general cases to particular cases. Only mathematical induction moves from particular cases to a general case and still remains a proof. To compare these three types of reasoning, we will look at the example Poincaré uses.

$a + 1 = 1 + a$ is a general theorem about any counting number a. For example, 2+1=1+2; 8+1=1+8. This theorem is called the commutative law of arithmetic. How is this theorem proved by mathematical induction? For any case we consider, we will have proved that a+1=1+a if beginning with this equation we pass through a series of logically justified steps and we end up with the equation a+1=1+a where the right and left sides of the equation are in every way identical. So to begin the proof, we check that the claim holds for the number 1 by substituting it in for a. When we do this we get 1+1=1+1 which immediately gives us the identity of the two sides of the equation. Now we assume that this claim holds for some number a which we will call n. So for a=n, we are assuming that a+1=1+a or n +1=1+n. Now we are called upon to use that assumption and perhaps the fact that 1+1=1+1 to show that it holds for the next number or when a=n+1.

The theorem we are trying to prove now states   (n+1)+1=1+(n+1).

We will prove this by rewriting the right side of the equation.

First we drop the parentheses to get   n+1+1=1+n+1

But we assumed that n+1=1+n, so we can rewrite the 1+n as n+1
Now our two sides are identical. $\qquad\qquad$ n+1+1=n+1+1
So we have proved the claim.

So since we have shown that this theorem holds for a =n+1 when it holds for a=n and we verified that it held for a=1, we now can show it holds for a=2. And because it holds for $a = 2$, it holds for $a = 3$ and so on. It therefore holds for all numbers. This is a proof by mathematical induction.

Poincaré presents this as the model of mathematical reasoning. Why is such a proof convincing, if it is? Poincaré states that we are entirely convinced because "this type of proof is an affirmation of the power of the mind which knows it can conceive of the infinite repetition of the same mental act when the act is once possible." But how does it know this? When you are certain of such a proof, do you feel confident that nothing will stop your mind from the same act in the future? But how do you know this? Is it because you have observed how your mind works? But isn't the experience of the mind working a certain way, or having a certain power, a normal case of induction from experience? There we say we could always reverse ourselves and even our best supported conclusions could be reinterpreted because of a new theoretical view of the evidence, as Newton's theory caused us to do with respect to weight. Poincaré claims it is not. Rather, he states we have direct immediate non-inductive knowledge that our minds can do this. He says we have a direct intuition of this power, and by performing this act when we read such a proof, we merely become aware of what we already know about ourselves. It is therefore immediately known without an inductive process. But then why couldn't we say the same about a +1=1+a?

TEXT

Poincaré: *Mathematical Induction*

How would we prove an arithmetic law for all whole numbers, for example, the law $a + 1 = 1 + a$ for all a? This is called the commutative law. The theorem is evidently true for $a = 1$; we can *verify* by purely analytical or logical reasoning that *if* it is true for $a = $ n, *then* it will be true for $a = $ n + 1. Now, it is true for a=1, and therefore is true for $a = 2$, $a = 3$, and so on. This is what is meant by saying that the proof is demonstrated "by induction". The whole process is a proof by the method of mathematical induction. We first show that a theorem is true for n = 1. We then show that, if it is true for n, it is true for n +1, the next number. Finally we conclude that it is true for all integers. This is therefore mathematical reasoning *par excellence,* and we must examine it more closely.

The essential characteristic of reasoning by induction is that it contains, condensed, so to speak, in a single formula, an infinite number of syllogisms. We shall see this more clearly if we enunciate the syllogisms one after another. They follow one another, if one may use the expression, in a cascade. The following are the hypothetical syllogisms: The theorem is true of the number 1. Now, if it is true of 1, it is true of 2; therefore it is true of 2. Now, if it is true of 2, it is true of 3; hence it is true of 3, and so on. We see that the conclusion of each syllogism serves as a premise of its successor. Further, the premises of all our syllogisms may be reduced to a single form. If the theorem is true of n, it is true of n+1.

It is now easy to understand why every particular instance of a theorem may be verified by purely logical and analytical processes. If, instead of proving that our theorem is true for all numbers, we only wish to show that it is true for the number 6, for instance, it will be enough to establish the first five demonstrations in our cascade. We shall require 9 arguments if we wish to prove it for the number 10. but however far we went we should never reach the general theorem applicable to all numbers, which alone is the object of science. To reach it we should require an infinite number of arguments, and we should have to cross an abyss that the patience of the mathematician, if restricted to the resources of formal logic, will never succeed in crossing.

I once asked why we cannot conceive of a mind powerful enough to see at a glance the whole body of mathematical truth. To prove even the smallest theorem we must use reasoning by induction, for that is the only instrument that enables us to pass from the finite to the infinite. This method of proof is always useful, for it enables us to leap over as many stages as we wish. It frees us from the necessity of long, tedious, and monotonous verifications, which would rapidly become impracticable. When we wish to prove the general theorem it becomes indispensable. Otherwise, we should ever be approaching the logical verification of particular cases without ever actually reaching the general truths. In this domain of arithmetic, the idea of mathematical infinity is already playing a preponderating part. Without it, there would be no science at all because there would be nothing general.

Reasoning by mathematical induction may be exhibited in other cases, and it may appear that we can justify this method of proof. We may say, for instance, that in any finite collection of different integers there is always one number that is smaller than others. In such cases, we may readily pass from one particular collection to another by mere logic, and thus give ourselves the illusion of having proved that reasoning by induction is legitimate. But we shall always be brought to a full stop – we shall always come to an indemonstrable axiom, which will at bottom be but the proposition we had to prove stated in different words. In this case we must assume the general truth that of two different numbers, one is less than the other. We cannot prove such a truth merely by logic. We cannot therefore escape the conclusion that the rule of reasoning by induction is irreducible to the principle of contradiction. Nor can the rule come to us from experiment. Experiment may teach us that the rule of induction is true for the first ten or the first hundred numbers. We could show that it always works for any claim which involves just those numbers. It will not bring us to the infinite series of numbers, but only to a more or less long, but always limited, portion of the series. Now, if such a limited series were all that is in question, the principle of contradiction would be sufficient. It would always enable us to develop as many particular syllogisms as we wished. It is only when it is a question of a single formula to embrace an infinite number of syllogisms that this principle breaks down, and there, too, experiment is powerless to aid. The rule that we have called mathematical induction is therefore inaccessible both to logical proof and to demonstration by experiment.

Why then is this type of argument imposed upon us with such an irresistible weight of evidence? It is because it is only the affirmation of the power of the mind, which knows it can conceive of the indefinite repetition of the same act, when the act is once recognized to be possible. The mind has a direct intuition of this power, and experiment can only be for it an opportunity of using it, and thereby of becoming conscious of it. It cannot escape our notice that here is a striking analogy with the usual processes of induction. But an essential difference exists.

Induction applied to the physical sciences is always uncertain, because it is based on the belief in a general order of the universe, an order that is external to us.

119

Mathematical induction is, on the contrary, necessarily imposed on us, because it is only the affirmation of a property of the mind itself.

Mathematicians, as I have said before, always endeavor to generalize the propositions they have obtained. To seek no further example, we have just shown the equality, $a + 1 = 1 + a$, and we could then use it to establish the equality, $a + b = b + a$, which is obviously more general. Mathematics may, therefore, like the other sciences, proceed from the particular to the general. This is a fact that might otherwise have appeared incomprehensible to us at the beginning of this study, but that has no longer anything mysterious about it, since we have ascertained the analogies between proof by mathematical reasoning and ordinary induction.

No doubt mathematical inductive reasoning and physical inductive reasoning are based on different foundations, but they move in parallel lines and in the same direction – namely, from the particular to the general. In contrast, purely logical processes leave us at the same level of generality we begin with. We can only ascend to more universal truths in mathematics by mathematical induction, for from it alone we can learn something new.

Diamond Painting in Red, Yellow, and Blue; Piet MONDRIAN; National Gallery of Art, Washington;
Gift of Herbert and Nannette Rothschild

Questions

1a. Listed below are various features of the painting. Which features suggest to you that the painting is incomplete?

	Suggests incompleteness	Does not suggest incompleteness
The lines		
The colors		
The shapes		
The way it is orientated		

1b. How would you complete it?

2. Why do we make generalizations from our experience?

3. Do you feel that mathematical induction is a legitimate form of proof, or do you feel it only gives you a high probability of truth? In other words, is it like scientific induction or is it as certain as any other type of mathematical proof?

Explain your answer.

XV

KNOWING THAT 1 + 1 = 2
TEXT: Russell, *Introduction to Mathematical Philosophy*

Orientation:

The natural numbers (0,1,2,3...) are the part of mathematics most familiar to people. We learn to use them before we reach school, and each of us has achieved a high level of expertise with them. It is rare to meet someone who has no ability to add, subtract, and multiply numbers they have never seen before. Few of us have ever had the occasion to use the natural numbers 4,814 and 18,111, and yet we have no trouble concluding that they add up to 22,925. Though we sometimes make mistakes, we do so out of carelessness. We do not make them out of ignorance. Presumably this is because we have spent years mastering a set of rules that we have little or no difficulty applying in any particular case. The question we will face in this unit is whether our knowledge of these particular rules needs to be improved in any way. One obvious answer is that a smaller number of rules is better than a larger number. If we could reduce a hundred rules to 5 or 10 rules, we would probably all feel that we had made progress. They would be easier to remember, and we could derive other rules as we needed them. But is there any other advantage which goes beyond the issue of the efficiency of our memories? Does it affect our understanding of the rules we learned through countless drills and practice? There are instances when we do, in fact, feel that this has occurred. When we see the numbers of a simple series like 1,2,4,8,16,..., we immediately infer that each term is generated by doubling the previous one. If we were asked, however, what the 32nd term is, we would not be able to answer without finding the 31st. Yet, if we had a rule for the series – in this case 2^{n-1}, where n is the place number of the term – we could describe any particular term without going through all the previous items. For example, suppose we wished to know the sixth term in this series. Since n=6, n-1 would equal 5 and we would use the rule for the series 2^{n-1} to find the result. In this case, that would be $2^5=32$. The sixth term is therefore 32. Here is a case where an underlying rule, or principle, helps, even when the answers produced are exactly the same. The question is whether there are deeper reasons for developing such rules or postulates or axioms to describe what we already know.

The mathematician, G. Peano, was the first to set down a set of five postulates

---

Bertrand Russell (1870-1970) was born in Trelleck, Wales, and taught at Cambridge University. He worked extensively in logic, mathematics, and the theory of knowledge. In 1913, he collaborated with A.N. Whitehead on *Principia Mathematica*. In addition, he was politically active throughout his life. His popular writings on politics, history of philosophy, and physics won him the Nobel Prize for Literature in 1950.

or axioms for whole number arithmetic. We will consider them in the version presented by Bertrand Russell. These postulates, when supplemented by some definitions of addition, subtraction, and multiplication enable us to *prove* all the other truths of arithmetic. The text states these rules, and uses them by sketching out a proof of 2 + 3 = 5. Would we, however, say that we know better or more fully that 2 + 3 = 5 after we read the proof than we did before we saw it? If a set of postulates proved that 3 + 2 did not equal 5, what would we say? Would we say that we made a new discovery about arithmetic, or would we throw out the postulates? In all probability, we would say that these statements are not postulates for arithmetic rather than claim that we now know that 3+2 does not equal 5. So it appears that when a mathematician produces postulates from which we can prove or derive a collection of truths, those postulates cannot violate the truths we already hold or the implications of those truths. But this assumes that we know and wholeheartedly accept these truths more strongly than the postulates.

Let us return to our previous example. Probably none of us has ever added 4,814 to 18,111. Suppose we had a proof from our postulates that 4,814 + 18,111= 22,935 instead of 22,925, the answer that we discovered by adding. Which would we believe, the postulates or our own rules of addition? Would we claim that numbers larger than 22,500 get strange, but that we hadn't previously noticed because we don't often use them? That claim would be hard to sustain. So again one asks why we should produce postulates if our previous knowledge of arithmetic and our experience with addition determines what qualifies as a postulate. To consider this issue, we bring up two kinds of cases where we possess a set of facts or truths, and yet seek for laws or rules from which we can derive what we already know. One such case is in science, the other concerns the law. These are not identical to the case of arithmetic, and the similarities and differences may assist us in focusing on the mathematical case.

In physics, theoreticians often attempt to produce a set of laws that account for a collection of data that were either previously observed (as in geology or astronomy), or produced in experiments (as in nuclear physics). When this is successful, scientists claim they understand the data they have. They claim they can *explain* the data. In addition, such a set of rules or laws often enables us to predict new experiences – Newton's theory of gravity enabled us to discover Uranus, Neptune, and Pluto. A scientific theory also often gives us a new way of looking at our experience – the orbit of planets around the sun and the fall of apples – we recognized to be rooted in something common. Our previous experience had to be re-interpreted. Before Newton, people viewed an object's weight as a primary characteristic of the object. After Newton, an object's mass replaced it as scientifically important, and weight became secondary. Weight was reinterpreted as the result of the acceleration caused by the attraction of the earth's mass on an object. When reading the postulates you should consider whether any of these features of scientific understanding have analogies with the postulates that concern the natural number system. Would the postulates allow us to *a)* unify certain kinds of truths, that seemed different, or *b)* predict new ones, or *c)* reinterpret a truth we already hold?

Another type of case deals with creations of human beings instead of with natural phenomena. Every society has hundreds of laws and customs regulating many aspects of daily life. Anthropologists, sociologists, judges, and legislators often study these laws to reduce them to a smaller number of fundamental laws. A famous instance of this procedure occurs in the New Testament. There, Christ states that the approximately 600 laws of the Old Testament are really summed up by two laws: Love your neighbor as yourself, and Love God with all your heart, soul and mind. This claim was not merely an aid to memory, but was a major step in transforming one religion into another. In more ordinary situations, the following often occurs. The Supreme Court decides that a particular case violates the Constitution. The court presents an opinion articulating the reason for its decision. This opinion spells out the principle which led to its decision. It will have consequences about what other laws are also now unconstitutional and will in addition set the tone for new laws passed by Congress and state legislatures. Does this type of case present analogies for mathematical postulates? Both of these examples - science and the law - may present only superficial suggestions and you may be able to think of more useful analogies. **(Read the text now, and then the remaining part of the orientation section.)**

The five Peano postulates for natural numbers are split into three types of claims: concerning the nature of 0, concerning the meaning of "successor" and concerning a rule of reasoning. Postulate #1 deals with a specific object of the arithmetic: it states that 0 is a number. The next three postulates consider the term "successor". Postulate #2 gives a rule to generate ever new numbers without any limit. One could ask how would one set a limit to the successor relation. How would one state a postulate for a number system in which there were only the numbers 0,1,2,3,4 and 5? Postulate #3 states that a number is the successor of only one number. In other words, 4 cannot be both the successor of 3 and also the successor of some other number, e.g., 11. If we define "predecessor of x" as the "number whose successor is x", then Postulate #3 states that the predecessor of a number x is unique. One question that emerges is whether a number has only one successor. For example, could the number 3 have both 4 and 11 as successors? Do these postulates exclude the possibility that a number has two successors? Do we need another postulate to eliminate this possibility? If a number had two successors, this number system would continually branch out. This would happen because, since two numbers cannot have the same successor, the branches would never unite. Postulate #4 returns to the number 0, and states that it is not the successor of some number.

This means that this number system has one boundary, 0. If we were creating postulate systems for numbers other than the natural numbers– for example, the positive and negative integers – then this postulate would have to be changed, since 0 would be the successor of some number, namely of -1. If on the other hand we were creating a postulate system for the finite set of numbers (0,1,2,3,4,5), we would have to make a number of decisions about the concept of successor. We could decide that 5 does not have a successor or perhaps decide that the number system circles back and that 0 is the successor of 5. Choosing one of the other postulates would yield very different kinds of number systems. In the former case, not every number would have a successor; in the latter, every number would have this relation to another. In the former case the successor of a number would always be greater than that number, but this would not be true in the latter case in which 0 is the successor of 5.

The last postulate presents a rule of reasoning for the arithmetic of natural numbers. It states if a certain characteristic holds of the first number, and if when it holds of a number n, it also holds of n's successor, or (n+1), then it holds of all numbers. For example, on Russell's formulation, this rule states that, if something is true of 0, and when true of 5, it is true of 6, then it is true of all numbers. This rule of reasoning is explored in detail in Unit XIV on Mathematical Induction. From the perspective of this lesson, one should consider whether such a rule of reasoning is a radically different kind of postulate from the others. Should a set of postulates only state the fundamental facts or truths of a particular subject matter or should it also inform us how to go about reasoning about them? Perhaps such a rule of reasoning should be part of a different subject matter – for example, Logic? Or do you think that our suggestion that the five postulates fall into three different groups is merely a useful organizing device to present them, and that in reality they are all rules of reasoning – some more general than others?

TEXT

Russell: *Peano's Postulates for Arithmetic, from Introduction to Mathematical Philosophy*

To the average educated person of the present day, the obvious starting-point of mathematics would be the series of whole numbers, 1,2,3,4, etc. Probably only a person with some mathematical knowledge would think of beginning with 0 instead of 1, but we will presume this degree of knowledge. We shall take as our starting-point the series: $0,1,2,3,...n,n+1$. It is this series that we shall mean when we speak of the "series of natural numbers".

It is only at a high stage of civilization that we could take this series as our starting-point. It must have required many ages to discover that a brace of pheasants and a couple of days were both instances of the number 2: the degree of abstraction involved is far from easy. And the discovery that 1 is a number must have been difficult. As for 0, it is a very recent addition; the Greeks and Romans had no such digit. The natural numbers seem to represent what is easiest and most familiar in mathematics. But though familiar, they are not understood.

Very few people are prepared with a definition of what is meant by "number", or "0" or "1". It is not very difficult to see that, starting from 0, any other of the natural numbers can be reached by repeated additions of 1. But we shall have to define what we mean by "adding 1", and what we mean by "repeated". These questions are by no means easy. It was believed until recently that some, at least, of these first notions of arithmetic must be accepted as too simple and primitive to be defined. Since all terms that are defined are defined by means of other terms, it is clear that human knowledge must always be content to accept some terms as intelligible without definition, in order to have a starting-point for its definitions. It is not clear that there must be terms that are *incapable* of definition. It is possible that, however far back we go in defining, we always *might* go farther still. On the other hand, it is also possible that, when analysis has been pushed far enough, we can reach terms that really are simple, and therefore logically incapable of the sort of definition that consists in analyzing. This is a question that it is not that, necessary for us to decide. For our purposes it is sufficient to observe since human powers are finite, the definitions known to us must always begin somewhere, with terms undefined for the moment, though perhaps not permanently.

All traditional pure mathematics, including analytical geometry, may be regarded as consisting wholly of propositions about the natural numbers. That is to say, the terms that occur can be defined by means of the natural numbers, and the propositions can be deduced from the properties of the natural numbers –with the addition, in each case, of the ideas and propositions of pure logic.

Having reduced all traditional pure mathematics to the theory of the natural numbers, the next step in logical analysis was to reduce this theory itself to the smallest set of premises and undefined terms from which it could be derived. This work was accomplished by Peano. He showed that the entire theory of the natural numbers could be derived from the three primitive ideas and five primitive postulates in addition to those of pure logic. These three ideas and five postulates thus became, as it were, hostages for the whole of traditional pure mathematics.

The three primitive ideas in Peano's arithmetic are: 0, number, successor. By "successor" he means the next number in the natural order. That is to say, the successor of 0 is 1, the successor of 1 is 2, and so on. By "number" he means, in this connection, the class of the natural numbers. He is not assuming that we know all the members of this class, but only that we know what we mean when we say that this or that is a number, just as we know what we mean when we say "Jones is a man," though we do not know all men individually.

The five primitive postulates that Peano assumes are:

(1) 0 is a number

(2) The successor of any number is a number.

(3) No two numbers have the same successor.

(4) 0 is not the successor of any number.

(5) Any property that belongs to 0, and also to the successor of every number that has the property, belongs to all numbers.

The last of these is the principle of mathematical induction.

Let us consider briefly the kind of way in which the theory of the natural numbers results from these three ideas and five postulates. To begin with, we define 1 as "the successor of 0", 2 as "the successor of 1", and so on. We can obviously go on as long as we like with these definitions, since, in virtue of (2), every number that we reach will have a successor, and, in virtue of (3), this cannot be any of the numbers already defined. If it were, two different numbers would have the same successor. In virtue of (4) none of the numbers we reach in the series of successors can be 0. Thus the series of successors gives us an endless series of continually new numbers. In virtue of (5), all numbers come in this series, which begins with 0 and travels on through successive successors: for (a) 0 belongs to this series, and (b) if a number *n* belongs to it, so does its successor, whence, by mathematical induction, every number belongs to the series.

Suppose we wish to define the sum of two numbers. Taking any number *m*, we define *m + 0* as *m*, and *m + (n + 1)* as the successor of *m+n*. In virtue of (5) this gives a definition of the sum of *m* and *n*, whatever number *n* may be. Similarly we can define the product of any two numbers.

Proof of 2+3=5 (adapted from Peano)

Definition 1: successor of n is n' ($1=0'$ $2=(0')'$ etc.).

Definition 2: $m +0=m$.

Definition 3: $m +k' = (m+k)'$. or (m plus the successor of k equals the successor of (m plus k)).

1.	$3+2=3+1'$	Def. 1
2.	$3+1' = 3+(0')'$	Def. 1
3.	so $3+2=3+(0')'$	
4.	$3 +(0')' = (3+0')'$	Def. 3
5.	$(3+0')' =((3+0)')'$	Def. 3
6.	so $3+2=((3+0)')'$	
7.	But $(3+0)=3$	Def. 2
8.	so $3+2=((3)')'$	
9.	But $3' =4$	Def. 1
10.	so $3+2=(4)'$	
11.	But $(4)' =5$	Def. 1
12.	so $3+2=5$	

Questions

1. Create a new set of postulates by denying one of the first four Peano postulates. This will create an arithmetic different from ours. State two truths in this new arithmetic. Give some examples.

2. a) State one way the Peano postulates are like the example from science (Newton), and one way they are like the examples from civil laws.

   b) State one way the Peano postulates are not like the science example, and one way they are unlike the example of laws.

XVI MATHEMATICAL MAPS AND MODELS
TEXT: Boole, *The Laws of Thought*

Orientation:

Maps and models play significant roles in our lives. As children we played with and learned from models – dolls, toy houses, trains, and planes. Almost every facet of daily life has been modeled by toys. Some models were built by us, some were already constructed for our use. In every case, as we played with them, we became familiar with the features they modeled. By exploring one object, we were able to learn about another. As we grow up and begin to travel, more complex models such as maps take on a crucial if not essential place in our activities. This is especially true for those of us who drive. Often, we would literally be lost without them. A world as complex and interconnected as ours would be inconceivable without maps and models. Our economic and social systems would collapse. Complex buildings, bridges, roads, and most machines could not be constructed without models. Without maps, the transportation and delivery system would crumble. Maps and models, however, are not indispensable only in practical activities. They have become equally essential in science and in mathematics. The questions that emerge are why we need such tools, how we construct them, and what the advantages and disadvantages of using them are.

Though maps and models tend to have different uses in everyday life, their fundamental structure is similar, if not identical. A model or a map reproduces some structural feature or features of one object in another object. A model of a train, for example, reproduces the shape and the interconnection of some of the parts of the vehicle we ride. A typical road map models a three dimensional terrain on the two dimensional surface of a sheet of paper. Though there are many kinds of maps, most of them are primarily concerned with showing the location of places and the distances between them. This is achieved by having the order of the towns on a road reproduced on the map by the identical ordering of points on a line. If the line represents the road, the points will represent the towns. Distance is dealt with by a scale: a certain length on a map represents a certain actual distance on the road – such as, 1 inch = 1 mile.

What this simple example illustrates is that we make choices whenever we model or map. Not every feature of the original object reappears in the model or

George Boole (1815 - 64) was born in Lincoln, England. He became Professor of Mathematics at Cork in Ireland in 1849. The principal creator of modern logic, his important works are *Mathematical Analysis of Logic* (1847), and his crucial work, *Laws of Thought* (1854).

130

map. The typical model or map is smaller than what is mapped, made of different materials, and involves our learning how to read or interpret it. The first two features are generally matters of convenience. In contrast, a DNA model is larger than a DNA molecule. A model of a space shuttle used on the ground by training astronauts is identical in size and materials to the one they will fly in. The issue of interpretation, however, is essential. For example, we had to learn that the different colors of countries on a world map are used to highlight their boundaries, and that they are not a depiction of the place of those countries in the visible spectrum. And of course modeling or mapping can be a symmetrical relation. If a globe is a map of the earth, the earth could be a model of the globe in our rooms. A giant whose body was the size of the distance between the earth and the moon could use the earth to model the globe in our classroom. The identity of structure goes in both directions. Which is the model and which is the object modeled depends on our purposes and our decisions. Learning to use and read models and maps is similar to learning a language. In fact, some thinkers have suggested that language itself is best understood as a model or map. If this is so, what would language aim to model or map – the world, our thoughts, our culture?

One of the first instances of modeling in mathematics was by George Boole, a 19th century logician and mathematician, who created the Boolean algebra. Boole investigated the laws of logic. He thought these laws make language possible, and could be discovered piecemeal by investigating what we must presuppose to use words and sentences meaningfully. Though these laws could be discovered individually, Boole faced the issue of how they could be interconnected. Since interconnecting the laws of logic by means of logic would be circular, he had to look elsewhere for assistance. He suspected, however, that the laws of algebra and arithmetic were very similar in structure to the laws of logic. If he could discover a part of algebra and arithmetic with a structure identical to the structure of logic, he could use that algebra to model logic. To do this, he created a variant arithmetic with only two numbers, namely 0 and 1. This arithmetic was governed by a set of laws describing how to multiply and add these numbers. If he could interpret the symbols and laws of this arithmetic as the symbols and laws of logic, he would have a model of logic. He could then use this arithmetical algebra to investigate and explore the interconnection of the laws of the logic, and even to discover new ones. The identity of structure between arithmetic and logic would be like the identity of shape between the earth and the globe – both are spheres. The interpretation of the symbols of logic as specific numbers would be like letting cities on the earth be represented by dots on the globe. The key steps here, as in every modeling or mapping, are to establish an identity of structure between the two objects, or subject matters, in the laws governing the symbols, and to interpret the symbols. Boole's work will enable us to

131

scrutinize these issues.

Boole claims that the fundamental law of logic and of all thinking is the law of identity. This law states that a thing or object is the same as itself. Clearly this is not a very informative remark. It is a statement we undoubtedly all accept and even wonder why it was made. This sense of being trivially true – of being true of everything – is a characteristic of logical truth. Since one can hardly think of something more trivially true, this statement is a good candidate for the most fundamental logical truth. An example of this truth is "A tree is a tree." Boole, however, chooses to represent this truth in an unusual form which he believes better captures what it claims. His example is "A tree tree is a tree." His thinking behind this strange choice is that if two objects are absolutely identical, they are not two objects but rather just one. Taking a specific tree twice gives you just what you started with – the same tree. If it doesn't, the trees were different.

Once Boole has formulated the law of identity in the form he thinks most revealing, he must decide how to represent it symbolically in a form more familiar to us, and so he uses the language of algebra to create his mode. If one thought that the law should be stated as "A tree is a tree," one would choose the algebraic form A=A. But since Boole chooses a different formulation – taking a thing twice gives you what you started with – his options are $A+A=A$ or $A\times A=A$; or $A^2 =A$. He chooses the latter form. How would you have chosen?

Once Boole has made the decision to use multiplication, he moves on to another question, What in arithmetic can represent the law $A^2 = A$? That law is the fundamental law of logic and Boole looks to find some aspect of arithmetic where that law holds a comparable position. $A^2 = A$ is true of only two numbers 0 and 1, since $0^2 = 0$ and $1^2 = 1$. In our normal arithmetic, 0 and 1 are simply two numbers among others. But, as we see here, they sometimes behave differently from others. Squaring them, unlike squaring other numbers, gives us what we started with. We could imagine these two numbers constituting an entire arithmetic and satisfying laws unique to themselves. The laws these two numbers satisfy alone, or with one another, can therefore be made to model the laws of logic: the structures will be identical.

The next step now runs back from arithmetic to logic. 0 and 1 are numbers in arithmetic. How can they be interpreted logically? The suggestion Boole argues for is that 0, looked at logically, is "nothing", and 1 viewed logically is the concept "everything" or "the universe of all things". He argues that such an interpretation is possible on the basis of an analysis of the algebraic truths $0 \times y = 0$ and $1 \times y = y$. Once he has done this, he must then construe "+" and "-". If we assume that A is some object, what is meant logically by (1-A) or (A-1)? If 1 is everything, these expressions mean what is left over once A is removed from that totality. Generally, this is expressed logically as "not A".

Once Boole has gone this far in creating the model, he can begin to use it. Boole started by claiming that identity was the fundamental law of logic and that logic is a description of our laws of thought. Other thinkers, Aristotle, for example, had claimed that the law of non-contradiction is more basic. Whichever is more basic, they are certainly interconnected. The question is how to bring out that interconnection in a clear way. Boole's model can achieve that simply.

He starts with $$A^2 = A$$

Then he treats it algebraically $$A^2 - A = A - A$$
$$A^2 - A = 0$$

Therefore, $$A(A - 1) = 0$$

What does this last equation state? When interpreted as a part of logic, it states that nothing is both A and not A, which is a version of the law of non-contradiction. We can see this also if we solve the equation. The solutions are $A=0$ and $A=1$. Interpreted logically this says that A is simultaneously nothing and everything, since that's what 0 and 1 represent in the model; the model shows the connection between the two laws simply and transparently. If we hadn't realized they were interconnected, the algebra enables us to discover that. We can now continue to discover more and more laws of this arithmetic, and each one would give us a model of a law of logic. This possibility is all based, however, on how we interpret the symbols of one subject as those of another. Are Boole's interpretations reasonable, or would you have made different decisions?

TEXT

Boole: *Laws of Thought*

There is not only a close analogy but an exact agreement between the operation of the mind in logic and in the particular science of algebra. Of course the laws of these two subjects must be determined independently of one another. Any agreement in their form or structure can only be established by comparison. To borrow the symbolism of algebra, and then assume that in logic the laws governing the use of these symbols will be the same would be a mere hypothesis. And even so, in each subject the meaning of these symbols remains apart and independent. In addition, the symbols or words and operations of logic are entirely determined by a single law – the law of identity. A word means the same as itself. A word combined with itself names just what each names separately. This law of identity governs our use of words and how we use them to think logically. The law and operations of algebra are not confined to this simple law. We must first decide how to represent this law of logic in symbols.

The combination of two verbal symbols – e.g., "green" and "tree" – as expressed in the form "xy" names the entire class of objects, "green trees", to which the names or qualities represented by x and y together apply. If each symbol independently signifies the same object, their combination signifies just what each word alone would signify. In such a case, we have xy=x. Since in the law of identity y has exactly the same meaning as x, we may replace y with x in the equation. We thus get xx=x. In common algebra the combination xx is more briefly represented by x . Let us adopt the same principle of notation here. How we express a particular succession or combination of mental operations or thoughts is arbitrary. The above equation then assumes the form x = x.

We must now occupy ourselves with various questions about how we have represented the law of identity. This law is the characteristic of the operations of the human mind with words in speaking and reasoning. It is not the principal or only characteristic of its special operations in arithmetic and algebra. How is it that it is proper and useful that the same symbols be used to represent two distinct systems of thought? The ground of this use cannot consist in the fact that the symbols have the same meaning. For in systems of thought as distinct as logic and arithmetic, the symbols have entirely different meanings. Logic deals with how we conceive all

134

classes of things, arithmetic concerns only their numerical relations. However, the forms and methods of any specific system of reasoning depend primarily on the laws to which the symbols themselves are subject. They depend only indirectly on what those symbols stand for. So we can use the same symbols to represent different systems of thought, provided that the meanings assigned to the symbols make the forms of the laws in each system identical and that the use of those symbols internal to each system remains consistent.

The verbal symbols in logic are subject to the law of identity whose expression is $x^2 = x$. Now of the symbols of arithmetic only two, 0 and 1, are subject to the same formal law. We know that $0^2 = 0$ and that $1^2 = 1$. The equation $x^2 = x$ when viewed algebraically has no other roots than 0 and 1. Hence, instead of comparing the formal agreement in laws between logic and arithmetic generally, it is more immediately suggested to compare the laws of logic with an arithmetic whose symbols of quantity admit only the values 0 and 1. Let us imagine an algebra whose symbols – its variables x,y, and z and its constants a,b, and c – will take either value 0 or 1 and only these values. The laws, axioms and the processes of such an algebra will be identical in form with the laws, axioms, and processes of logic.

We must now determine the meaning in logic of the arithmetical symbols 0 and 1. The symbol 0 in algebra satisfies the formal law $0y = 0$ whatever number y may represent. In logic we think about classes of objects – *all* trees, *all* men, *all* etc. What class is represented by 0 so that whatever class y represents, the class 0y is identical with the class represented by 0? A little consideration will show that this condition is satisfied if the symbol 0 represents the class "Nothing". Whatever class y may be, the individuals common to both it and the class "Nothing" (a class which has no members), are the same as those contained in the class "Nothing". The law 0y =0) is satisfied only if 0 means the class "Nothing". In algebra, the symbol 1 satisfies the law $1y = y$ whatever number y represents. If 1 and y in logic represent classes, the law states that the individuals common to any class y and the class 1 are the individuals in class y. A little consideration will show that 1 must be the class of all objects – everything in the universe of things. Only this class must contain, as a part of it, all the individuals contained in any particular class y. Hence in logic, the meanings of 0 and 1 must be "Nothing" and the "Universe."

With the idea of any class of objects – for example, *men* – the contrary class of objects which are *not men* comes to mind. How do we represent this contrary class – the class of *not-men?* The whole universe is made up of these two classes together, since of every individual we can affirm that it is either a man or not a man. For greater distinctness, let x represent the class *men* and not-x the class of *not-men*. The Universe is represented by 1, and x and not-x represent *men* and *not-men*. Since everything in the universe is either a man or not a man, we represent this by x and not-x = 1, or not-x = 1 - x. This is the class which results when the class of men is removed from the class of all objects or the Universe. The contrary class *not-men* is therefore represented by 1-x.

PROPOSITION

The axiom that is termed the principle of contradiction, and that affirms that it is impossible for any being to possess a quality, and at the same time not to possess it, is a consequence of the fundamental law of thought, whose expression is x =x.

Let us write this equation in the form
$$x-x =0,$$
whence we have $x (1-x) = 0$. **(1)**

Let us, for simplicity of conception, give to the symbol x the particular interpretation of *men*, then 1 - x will represent the class of *not-men*. Now the formal product of the expressions of two classes represents that class of individuals that is common to them both. Hence x(1-x) will represent the class whose members are at once *men*, and *not men*, and the equation (1) thus expresses, as a principle, *that a class whose members are at the same time men and not men equals the class "Nothing".* In other words, that *it is impossible for the same individual to be at the same time a man and not a man.* Now let the meaning of the symbol x be extended from the representing of men, to that of any class of beings characterized by the possession of any quality whatever. The equation (1) will then express that it is impossible for a being to possess a quality and not to possess that quality at the same time. But this is the same as that "principle of contradiction" that Aristotle has described as the fundamental axiom of all existence. This proposition has been introduced as an illustration of a significant fact in the science of logic. What has been commonly regarded as the fundamental axiom of how things exist is but a consequence of a law of thought, when this law is represented in a mathematical form.

Questions

1. Look at the map on the front cover of the volume – you will need a magnifying glass to inspect the various levels. What does each level represent, and why did you interpret it that way? For what sort of journey do you think such a map would be useful?

2. Numbers are used to model the relations among many objects in the world. In the cases listed below, which purely arithmetic properties of numbers still hold in the model? The arithmetic properties are "greater than", "as much more than", and "so many times greater". In some of these uses of number, all of these hold, and in some, one or two of these properties remain true in the model.

A greater than B	A is as much more	A is so
B greater than C	than B as B is of C	many times
A is greater than C		greater than C

a) Person A has an IQ of 150.
   Person B has an IQ of 125.
   Person C has an IQ of 100.

b) The temperature is 100°C.
   The temperature is 50° C.
   The temperature is 0° C.

c) Team A is ranked fourth.
   Team B is ranked eighth.
   Team C is ranked twelfth.

d) The table is 20 inches long.
   The table is 15 inches long.
   The table is 10 inches long.

e) The stone weighs 10 lbs.
   The stone weighs 5 lbs.
   The stone weighs 0 lbs.

3. List six different characteristics of the human mind. Make a map of them that represents some of their interrelations. For example, you might use a circle. If you think our senses are the most important way we connect with the world you might start this way.

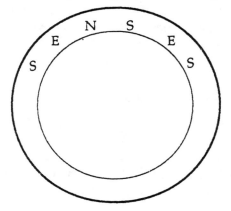

If you think our desires or needs occupy this role, one of these might occupy the outermost circle – if, that is, the map you decide is appropriate is circular.

138

APPENDIX

Some classes will probably not work through the entire volume sequentially, either because of time constraints or because they wish to focus on particular topics. This section will help a teacher make those choices. Each unit is briefly summarized and its relation to possible shorter sequences indicated. At the end of the Appendix, units are listed under specific topic headings: Geometry, Algebra, Mathematics and Science, Mathematical Thinking, Mathematics and Logic, and Proof. Each list contains the units most relevant to those topics.

Unit I. IS IT JUST A MATTER OF DEFINITION? The role of definitions is a key topic in mathematics and in other activities. Whether everything is definable, and what a definition should look like, are issues all students should consider. This unit would be a good introduction to any sequence.

Unit II. DO WE CREATE NUMBERS? This unit presents a view of mathematics as a creative activity. It allows exploration of underlying reasons for negative numbers, and can be extended into a justification for rational, real, and imaginary numbers. It is also a useful vehicle for considering the different forms that creativity takes in various fields.

Unit III. METAPHORS IN MATHEMATICS. Using the subject of the infinite, the unit focuses on the formation of concepts in mathematics. It first considers how metaphors are employed in the extension of a concept, and then how a new literal use might be established. The unit can be done at any point in the use of the book, but it should come before Unit VII on Cantor's proof.

Unit IV. ARE ONLY SOME PEOPLE GOOD AT MATH? Raises the question of what constitutes mathematical ability, and why some people are afraid of mathematics. At some stage in the use of the volume, this unit should be discussed by students. If the units are not done in sequence, this unit should be done after the class has had at least two or three sessions on other issues.

Unit V. STARTING TO THINK MATHEMATICALLY. This lesson introduces readers to the importance of postulates and axioms in mathematics, and starts the consideration of what a proof is. This can be done at any stage in the year, but could usefully come after the unit on definitions. It is a good introduction to the further discussion of axioms in Hilbert and Russell.

Unit VI. DEMONSTRATING THE UNPROVABLE. The status of logic – especially the law of Non-Contradiction – is examined. It raises such questions as, How do we discover logic? and, How confident should we be about logical truth? This should not be the first reading, and could usefully precede Unit X on mathematical truth, and Unit XVI on the logical law of Identity.

Unit VII. TALKING ABOUT THE INFINITE. This unit explores a disagreement about the mathematical concept of the infinite and about the method of proof employed in regard to it. The questions deal both with mathematics and with language. Since the students will probably take opposite sides on these issues, this unit should wait until your group has developed some skill at discussion.

Unit VIII. HOW DO YOU SAY "I LOVE YOU" IN ARITHMETIC? The utility of mathematics as a model for other subjects is investigated. The unit concentrates on a specific proposal for the creation of a perfect language based on arithmetic. Wider issues of the applicability of mathematics to daily activities can easily come up for discussion.

Unit IX. LOGICAL EQUIVALENCE IN MATHEMATICS. The concept of logical equivalence is examined using Euclid's Fifth, or Parallel, Postulate. By considering the criteria for choice among mathematically equivalent statements, this unit also raises questions of the diverse ways mathematics is used. It should be done after an introduction to postulates and axioms using Unit V.

Unit X. HOW ARE MATHEMATICAL TRUTHS TRUE? Mathematical truths are compared with truths in science and in logic to determine whether they are a unique type. Three major characteristics of mathematics are proposed for examination, and these set the context for discussion of the nature of mathematics. The unit can be extended to the issue of the role of experience and pure thought in mathematics. Students should have read and discussed Unit VI on non-contradiction before this unit.

Unit XI. BEYOND THE IMAGINATION. The status of alternative systems of mathematics is investigated using the creation of non-Euclidian geometry. The role in mathematics of intuition, imagination, and experience is examined. In addition, how to determine logical and mathematical possibility, and whether a system of mathematics is true or false, is considered. Students should have read Unit IX before doing this unit.

140

Unit XII. IT'S AXIOMATIC. This unit deals with the centrality of axioms in mathematics. It examines whether everything required in mathematics should be stated explicitly, and whether this is possible. The importance and problems caused by diagrams and definitions are treated. This unit could follow work with Unit I on definitions, and Unit VI on geometrical postulates.

Unit XIII. PHYSICAL MATHEMATICS AND MATHEMATICAL PHYSICS. This unit specifically compares the difference between mathematics and physics by investigating Newton's fusion of the two subject matters. This issue is then extended into the wider question of when it is fruitful to obscure the boundaries that appear to separate two subjects. Examples from the school curriculum are raised in order to explore this issue in familiar and concrete circumstances. The general question is quite accessible, but Newton's treatment is complex and should be done after the students have had experience with the Touchstones approach.

Unit XIV. LEAPING TO THE UNIVERSAL. Mathematics, science, and ordinary judgment move from particular cases to general claims by means of an inference called "induction". This movement of thought is considered by using a painting by Mondrian. The focus of this unit is then the differences between scientific and mathematical induction. These differences are made explicit and then compared. Mathematical induction is examined as a form of mathematical proof, equal in status to logical demonstrations and proofs previously examined. Students should have already discussed Unit V and Unit XII.

Unit XV. KNOWING THAT $1 + 1 = 2$. This unit investigates why we attempt to prove what we already know. It does this by exploring Peano's five axioms for arithmetic. The search for postulates to ground arithmetic truth is compared with the search for fundamental principles in science and in the law. In addition, students create variant arithmetics by modifying the Peano postulates.

Unit XVI. MATHEMATICAL MAPS AND MODELS. The strategy of using models in mathematics and science is explored. This investigation uses the first effort at modeling, which is Boole's use of an arithmetic of only two numbers as a model for logic. The general question of how we learn from models and the extent of their use can be addressed. In addition, questions of the details of modeling come up, specifically concerning how to interpret objects in one subject matter, or area of study, as objects in a model.

For teachers who desire to use this volume to consider particular topics, the following sequences are recommended.

Geometry
Unit I
Unit V
Unit IX
Unit XI
Unit XII

Algebra
Unit II
Unit VII
Unit XIV
Unit XV
Unit XVI

Mathematical Thinking
Unit III
Unit IV
Unit VII
Unit XIV
Unit XVI

Mathematics and Logic
Unit I
Unit V
Unit VI
Unit IX
Unit X
Unit XVI

Proof
Unit V
Unit VI
Unit VII
Unit XII
Unit XIV

Mathematics and Science
Unit II
Unit III
Unit X
Unit XIII
Unit XIV

INDEX

144